CONFIDENCE IN GOD,

THE

ONLY TRUE REST FOR THE SOUL,

AND

REFUGE IN THESE ALARMING TIMES.

" We have known and *believed* the love that God hath to us."
1 John iv. 16.

" We, which have *believed*, do enter into rest."
Hebrews iv. 3.

LONDON:

J. HATCHARD AND SON, 187, PICCADILLY.

1840.

CONTENTS.

CHAPTER I.

Rest and peace, shown to be indispensable to the minds of
men - - - - - - - - - *Page* 1

CHAPTER II.

Man's natural want of it, and ceaseless craving after it, stated
and explained - - - - - - - 24

CHAPTER III.

The remedy for this, shown from Scripture - - 51

CHAPTER IV.

Objections to this remedy met and answered - - 73

CHAPTER V.

A further explanation of the subject - - - 103

CHAPTER VI.

The blessed effects of this remedy on our feelings towards
  God   -   -   -   -   -   -   -   -   - 140

CHAPTER VII.

Blessed effects of it on our feelings towards man   - 187

CHAPTER VIII.

Conclusion. A recapitulation of the whole   -   - 218

CONFIDENCE IN GOD.

CHAPTER I.

ONE of the strongest feelings of the human heart, of which we are all conscious, is the desire of mental ease and comfort. It is a fact amounting to proverbial notoriety, that without it a paradise of beauty may bloom around us in vain; and that with it, a dungeon may be transformed into a palace.

However in youth we may seek our pleasure in the more exciting, and in age in the serener, enjoyments of life; still a mind at ease is considered an indispensable ingredient in the cup of human happiness. While the reverse is regarded as the greatest aggravation of our distress: "the spirit of a man may sustain his infirmity; but a wounded spirit, who can bear?" Of all the good gifts this world has it in its power to bestow, *this* it never can con-

B

fer; as it is an inward frame of mind which is independent of all outward circumstances, that can of itself mar all our joy, or master all our grief.

> " The mind is its own place, and in itself
> Can make a heaven of hell, a hell of heaven."
> Milton.

And if even happiness below may be produced by a confluence of fortunate circumstances, the world which gave it to us may, " at one fell swoop," in a moment deprive us of it all. Nor can it even ensure the permanency of any part of it. Trite and common-place as this truism may appear, still, as nothing brings out opposites like the power of contrast, it may be allowed to have weight in an attempt to prove that the solid lasting peace which this world cannot give, Religion offers to bestow, promising to prove not only a perennial fount within us of joy and comfort, springing up into everlasting life, but to pour its healing streams over the barren and arid wastes of this world's disappointed hopes and blasted joys, so as to make the wilderness of despair " rejoice and blossom like the rose."

Since it is a truth, then, which every day's experience confirms, that " man is born to trouble as the sparks fly upwards," of what consequence is it for all to possess a principle capable of affording us a remedy for all these ills? But though, perhaps, there never was a time when the knowledge of religion was more extensively diffused or more universally professed ; still it must be obvious to all, that such happy effects are by no means so inseparable an attendant upon its progress, as to make the reception of religion and peace of mind synonymous terms ; as it is a subject of common complaint on the part of the candid, and a truth too plainly evidenced by the temper and feelings of many less open on the subject, that they do *not* find religion produce on their minds that happy effect, or exercise over them that powerful control which it was its distinguishing feature at its first promulgation to achieve.

That this cannot be the fault of religion, we have only to open our Bible to be assured of. As we there read our Lord's blessed promise, " Peace I leave with you, my peace I give unto you ; not as the world giveth, give *I* unto you," (John xiv. 27.) And by the apostle St. Paul we are assured, " that sin shall not have dominion over us, who are not under the law, but under grace," (Rom. vi. 14 ;) for that " the Gospel is the power of God unto salvation to every one that believeth," (ch. i. ver. 16 ;) therefore, every one in whom it has fallen short of accomplishing these grand ends, cannot be in possession of the *real* truths of the Gospel, or must be able to find in themselves some palpable and self-evident explanation of the reason why they are

defrauded of the inalienable legacy our Lord be-
queathed to all who should become his disciples.
This low state of things in common experience,
though it often admits of the simplest solution by
merely pointing at the life and habitual conduct of
the individual—" For he that saith, I know him,
and keepeth not his commandments," saith St. John,
" is a liar, and *the truth is not in him*;" yet, in so
many cases, arises from a cause in which they are
more to be pitied than blamed; namely, a perverted
view of the truths given to us by him, " who was
anointed to preach good tidings to the meek, to
bind up the broken-hearted, to proclaim liberty to
the captives, and the opening of the prison to them
that are bound, to proclaim the acceptable year of
the Lord, and to comfort all that mourn," (Isa. lxi.
1, 2;) that before we proceed to advert to cases
where the blame rests with the persons themselves,
we would endeavour to apply a remedy to yet commoner cases, where " those faces are made sad, that
God would not have made sad;" (Ezek. xiii. 22;) by
a mistaken apprehension, or defective knowledge of
the truths of the Gospel. Though " knowledge
has increased," according to Daniel's prediction of
these latter days, the tide has not deepened as it
has widened, a large proportion of people learning
only so much of the fear of God as to keep them at
a distance from all comfortable communion with

Him, or only so much of his love as, by instilling
a false idea of his benevolence, lulls their conscience
into an unsafe reliance upon his mercy, while their
conduct affords no grounds to warrant such a confidence ; for " whosoever doeth not righteousness is
not of God," (1 John iii. 10 ;) and only if our heart
condemn us, then have we confidence with him."
(verse 21.)

The very advantages the present generation possess, of cheap and widely-circulated religious publi-
cations, is injurious to it, in some respects, from its
allowing of a shallow acquaintance with the subject
of religion to be gained by all, while a sound understanding of its truth is attained by few. In place of
every one having to search for it themselves in Holy
Writ, as in a mine for silver, and seek for it by earnest study as for hid treasure, as the wise man
advises, (Prov. ii. 4,) and any knowledge that
people attained at all being thus necessarily elemen-
tary and deep, they are now-a-days inundated with
a deluge of diluted theology, in which all funda-
mental principles are taken for granted, and so left
untaught; and hence they are filled with a quantity
of vague, indistinct, and confused notions on the
subject, which not only are incapable of producing
those effects they expected upon their minds, but,
by deluding them into the idea they possess a thing
of which they talk and think and read so much, pre-

vents them seeking after purer light, or sinks them
into a state of absolute dejection, from the idea that
they have even sought in religion in vain for a cure
for their discomfort, which, of all causes of woe, is
the most cruel and the most insupportable; as it shuts
them out of the city of refuge which God has provided for all mourners, and deprives them of " that
river, the streams whereof make glad the holy place
of the tabernacle of the Most Highest;" and too
often proves, as it is deemed, the most fatal of all
mental maladies, from a notion that it is incurable.

And no wonder : for if it were possible to *conceive* that there was no balm in Gilead, no Physician *there* skilful enough to undertake the case, or
that the skill and efficacy of both had failed, well
might the malady be considered hopeless !

But the failure of a spurious medicine is no proof
of the inefficacy of the true ; and in a case like this,
where the very application of the remedy seems to
aggravate the disease, men, in place of seeking in
their religion for a remedy of their distress, should
seek to have their religion remedied. In all these
instances of the supposed failure of religion to accomplish what it has undertaken to do, we may
safely set the promises of God—" I, even I, am he
that comforteth thee"—" As one whom his mother
comforteth, so will I comfort thee," against the experience or the assertions of man to the contrary ;

being fully persuaded, that he who says, " Come unto me, all ye that labour and are heavy laden, and I will give you rest," is *able* to " give the oil of joy for mourning, the garment of praise for the spirit of heaviness," to " *all* those who are afflicted, tossed with tempest, and not comforted; and we may say, therefore, with confidence, to every mourner, whatever their cares may be, or from whatever cause they proceed, if the medicine of the Gospel has failed hitherto to effect a cure ; nay, if even, after applying to it, you feel, like the poor disappointed expectant from human aid in the Gospel, " Nothing bettered, but rather the worse," for the trial ; " listen not to an evil heart of unbelief that would tempt thee to doubt the truth of God's sacred word, that has assured thee of a cure : listen not to the suggestions of any who would lead thee to think there is a wound too desperate for God to heal—a cloud too dark to be " dispersed at the brightness of the rising of the dayspring from on high, to visit all who are in darkness and in the shadow of death. Listen only to the voice of God, however deep thy despondency may be, or however extreme its cause —though tribulation may have overflowed thy heart, and swept away every earthly comfort—though it may have covered over in the silent grave the lifeless form of every one you held dear on earth, may have deprived you of health, home, and property

nay, even of your good name, " whose price is above
rubies ;" yea, though life itself may be threatened ;
" yet the mountains may depart, and the hills be removed, but *my* kindness shall not depart from thee,
neither shall the covenant of my peace be removed,
saith the Lord, that hath mercy on thee." And should
this present little volume prove as incompetent to
convey the consolation you desire to your heart, as
all other attempts have done, be assured the blame
must rest with the writer, not with the subject,
which is one, indeed, more worthy of an angel's
tongue than of the pen of a poor fellow mortal. Be
not discouraged at this failure, and give up all further search, in the conviction that the Almighty has
raised hopes in the human heart he will fail to rea-
lize, for the fault must rest with the creature, not
with the Creator. " If we believe not *He* abideth
faithful, he cannot deny himself," who hath said,
" Peace, peace to him that is afar off, and to him that
is near, and I will heal him." But laying hold of the
sacred clue the promises of Scripture put into your
hand, let it not out of your grasp till it has guided
you out of the labyrinth of error you must be in, if
you do not see cause to " rejoice in the Lord alway ;" till it has lifted you out of the horrible pit—
out of the mire and clay, and set your feet upon a
rock, and put a new song in your mouth, even
thanksgiving unto our God."

But it stands to reason, it must be a comfortable religion in itself that we embrace ere it can be fitted to convey comfort in tribulation ; for if we bring into the house of mourning a principle by which " all joy has been darkened " in the house of prosperity, it is more calculated to increase than to dispel the gloom of such a scene. The sunshine of the breast must habitually illuminate the mind, or its rays will never prove strong enough to disperse the shades which surround that house, where sickness, sorrow, or death, have entered.

For be it remembered, religion affords us no exemption from the common calamities of life, it only offers us alleviation under them: it promises to throw no shield over the heart that embraces its truths. Nay, it warns us, becoming Christians, introduces us to a new species of trials even, and to many with which the world around us will remain unacquainted ; but it provides for *all* an ample, full, and sufficient remedy, so that they shall even be enabled to exclaim, " It is good for me to have been afflicted."

It is, perhaps, to be lamented, that the common style of comfort addressed to persons in a disconsolate state of mind, both from the press and the pulpit, is oftener more an attempt to comfort them under it than to rouse them out of it—trying to reconcile them to it, as a dispensation proceeding from the

sovereign pleasure of God, or as arising from some
fect in their natural temperament, or as a part of
that mysterious portion of trial allotted to us on
earth ; in place of showing them, that as the call of
the Gospel is, " Rejoice in the Lord alway, and
again I say, rejoice ;" and as the provision is so fully
suited to meet the demand, as to render the require-
ment for our doing so a most reasonable one on the
part of God, and a most practicable one on our part,
nay, one who is not complying with it is dishonouring
God, and defeating his gracious purposes towards
them by defrauding him of " the honour due unto
his most holy name." But some go so far, indeed,
as to say, that not only is comfort of mind no way
necessary for our well-being, or essential to our safety,
but that it is often purposely withheld for our benefit,
to advance us in holiness by promoting humility, and
insure our safety by increasing our diligence in the
use of the means of grace and performance of all
our duties, in the hope it may flow to us from this
source ; and all unite in assuring us, that it will be
bestowed at the time when we most need it—the
hour of death. However, for wise purposes, it may
be withheld now, so that it has passed into a proverbial expression, " Comfort is kept for a dying
day." " Miserable comforters are ye all," who
would thus leave us to our sorrow, or bid us be contented under it ! Not so did he who said, " I will

not leave you comfortless; I will come to you!"
But what is still more remarkable is, that many suf-
ferers seem to prefer this mode of comforting them,
to any attempt to raise them out of their sad condition, by showing them they are in any way so concerned in its removal as to be in a great measure
responsible for its continuance; and that they are
bringing discredit on their profession, and robbing
God of his glory, "because they serve not the
Lord their God with joyfulness and with gladness
of heart for the abundance of all things," (Deut.
xxviii. 47;) and claim instead, our sympathy, if not
our admiration of their patient acquiescence under
it, regarding the appointment rather as a badge of
distinction than as a brand of reproach, strangely
conceiving, because presumption and false confidence is a sin, distrust of God is a virtue. Let it
not be thought that this has any reference to actual
disease, over which we are no more bound to expect
the Almighty will choose to exercise his power for
relief, than even any *other* malady to which the
human frame is subject, though both are alike within his province to heal. Could it, indeed, be proved
that comfort and peace of mind were gifts conferred
by God, with no reference to the conduct of the
person they were given to, and independent of any
principles they had embraced, or which were in
operation in their practice, instead of being the

necessary consequence of our embracing certain
blessed truths, which possessed in themselves an
inherent power " to minister to a mind diseased,"
or overwhelmed by affliction ; calming every excited
passion, soothing every irritated feeling, and bracing
every nerve to a superhuman fortitude of endurance ; *then*, indeed, this forlorn state of gloomy
desertion into which many are plunged, would be a
call for heartfelt commiseration on our parts, and
for profound submission on their own, instead of
being an occasion for us to exhort them " to lift up
the hands which hang down, and to strengthen the
feeble knees." But, as we are firmly persuaded
this is not the case, we entreat of such to examine
themselves, " whether they are in the faith " of
that truth " which is all joy and peace in believing," " to prove their ownselves, that they may
have rejoicing in themselves alone, and not in another." We would ask them, whether it does not
appear likely, that the principles which are so confidently relied on as fully able to afford us all the
comfort and support we stand in need of in the hour
of nature's greatest extremity, must not be able
also to afford us supplies sufficient for the ordinary
and lesser trials and duties of life ? since they are
the very same principles, and are to undergo no alteration, which we are depending upon to effect
these far greater ends; for we all know we are to

have no new revelation, no fresh addition to the
supplies of grace so amply bestowed upon us already : we shall have no greater fund placed within
our reach at the hour of death, or at the day of
judgment, than is at this present moment granted to
us ; and if so, why should we postpone our desire of
relief to that season, and deprive ourselves of all the
benefits and advantages of its cheering and inspirit-
ing influence all the intermediate time that inter-
venes, and prefer living on hope to living in possession of the blessing?

Can we be considered free from *folly* in so doing,
when it is within our power, even if we could be
proved as free from blame in neglecting a point in
which the highest interests of our soul are involved,
as well as the glory of our Maker ? For may there
not be some danger, that the principles which have
been found insufficient to produce these lower ends,
may be found inadequate to achieve a greater ? and
that a life of dissatisfied uneasiness with our spiritual state, and of gloomy apprehension as to our
eternal prospects, may terminate in a dark and
dreary deathbed ?—if, indeed, its evils terminate
there—for such a state of uncertainty, doubt, and
distrust, seems anything but like that " kingdom of
heaven within us," which is righteousness and peace
and joy of the Holy Ghost,"—that identifies us, even
here, in a low degree, (the church militant and hu-

miliated,) with the church glorified above, which
" rests not day nor night," singing praises to
God. But sad as this want of comfort is even, it is
not perhaps the worst evil which may befall us, in
consequence of our possessing a shallow knowledge
of the life-giving truths of the Gospel. We are warned, that with an increase of knowledge at the last
day was to be also an increase of temptation, (Dan.
xi. 35;) and that, in consequence, " *many should
fall*," to try them and to purge them; " and that
the false prophets that should arise would deceive
many, insomuch that even, if it were possible, the
very elect." And that, " because iniquity should
thus abound, the love of many should wax cold.
And to such an *extent* would this defection and apostasy go, that our Lord seems to think it even possible faith might perish from the earth nearly ; and
adds, " Nevertheless, when the Son of man cometh, shall he find faith upon the earth ?" So much,
and so many things, should occur to sap the belief,
and thin the ranks of Christians, that few, he fore-
tells, would reap the glorious rewards promised to
him that overcometh. (Rev. i, ii, iii.) And they who
discern the signs of the times, must see that " that
hour is near, even at the door ;" when not only are
the outward walls of Zion attacked by infidels, who
seek to break down the carved work thereof with the
axes and hammers of revolutionary reform, " crying,

Down with it, down with it, even to the ground;"
and when many of the watchmen, placed by her
upon her walls for her defence, have joined in league
with the assailants, and are lending their aid in her
destruction by avowing those latitudinarian principles which have for their object the subversion of
every established church in the land, and to let in
the flood-tide of liberalism and confusion into our
universities and churches. Nay, when treason is
introduced into the very citadel itself by the arti-
fices of evil men and evil spirits, which the fanati-
cism that sprang up in the bosom of the one establishment in the land, and the semi-popery issuing
from the cloisters of the other, bear witness to.
And when, last of all, and *worst* of all, Socinianism,
like a creeping palsy, is insidiously benumbing many
limbs of the church established among us, has un-
christianized whole bodies of dissenters, as it seems
to threaten to do the whole continent of the New
World, it behoves us to look to ourselves, to see if
we are " so rooted and grounded in the faith of
Christ, and so uninfected with the prevailing
errors of the day, that we may lean confidently upon
the promise of our Redeemer: "Because thou hast kept
the word of my patience, I also will keep thee from
the hour of temptation that is to try them that dwell
upon the earth.'' And we should recollect that St.
Paul tells us, the only way to prevent " our being

tossed to and fro, and carried about by every wind
of doctrine, by the sleight of man and cunning craf-
tiness, whereby they lie in wait to deceive," is " to
be no longer children, but to grow up unto Christ
in all things, till we come in the unity of the Spirit,
and of the knowledge of the Son of God, unto a perfect man—unto the measure of the stature of the
fulness of Christ." And it is a fact worth reflection,
that the majority of those who have lent an ear to the
seductive arguments of these parties, are those who
were dissatisfied with the effects which they found
their already received religious opinions had produced upon them, and who, struck with the high
tone of the sanctifying and elevating nature of these
new doctrines its teachers assumed, hoped vainly
they were to be shown by them a more excellent
way : when, had they been filled with all joy and
peace in believing, as they were well entitled *to*
expect to be, from the power of true religion upon
their minds, they would " have had the witness
in themselves" that they *possessed* the pearl of
great price, and therefore needed to search no
more for it ; and would have been less in the way of
temptation had any one said, " Come with us, and we
will do thee good." And if, as succeeding these days
of danger to the faith of Christ's disciples, there is to
be a time of trouble, such as never has been on the
earth from the foundation of the world, neither again

shall there be any like it, as all writers on prophecy conspire to warn us, we have an additional reason for standing firm, being stedfast and immovable; and for examining ourselves, and proving ourselves, and " taking to us the whole armour of God, that we may be able to withstand in the evil day ; and having done all, to stand ;" " praying always, with all prayer and supplication in the Spirit, that the God and Father of our Lord Jesus Christ, the Father of glory, may give unto us the spirit of wisdom and of revelation in the knowledge of him ; the eyes of our understanding being enlightened, that we may know what is the hope of his calling," and " may continue in the faith, grounded and settled, and be not moved away from the hope of the Gospel."

Did we place religious knowledge upon the same footing with any *other* species of knowledge, we should consider the mere enlightening of the intellect upon the subject would go a very little way in effecting any powerful influence upon the life : as we see men totally change their opinions upon all other subjects, without its making any alteration in their conduct : but as the Gospel is declared to be " the power of God," as well as " the wisdom of God," and that instrument by which the Omnipotent accomplishes the most stupendous effects by means apparently the most insignificant and unfitted for the purpose ; and as we are told, every one " who

c

receives into an honest and good heart the incorruptible word of life, which is able to save their souls," it will effectually work in all them that believe, to the saving of their souls,—we must regard the right understanding and proper reception of it as indispensable to salvation, and every addition to our knowledge of it, a fresh accession of strength to the soul. And though it is, alas! an undoubted fact, that the knowledge may be in us without the power, " the letter which killeth the Gospel even," without " the Spirit which giveth life." And " like to a man beholding his natural face in a glass, and that goeth his way, and straightway forgetteth what manner of man he was;" so we, too, by yielding a mere intellectual assent to it, may think that we know all things, when we know *nothing* yet, as we ought to know. But though the knowledge may be in us thus without the power, the power never can be in us without the knowledge; many may possess hoards of false coin, and not be rich : yet none can be rich unless they possess the true coin : therefore, though some may " receive the truth to no profit, save the subverting of the hearers, we should not be discouraged from pressing it, for this reason, upon any, " being instant in season and out of season." " For faith cometh by hearing, and hearing by the word of God." Supported by the promise, " Cast thy bread upon the waters, for thou shalt find it after many days," and

guided by the command, " He that *hath* my word,
let him speak my word faithfully ; for what is the
chaff to the wheat ? saith the Lord." (Jer. xxiii. 28.)
To a mind, indeed, sinning against light, trifling
with sin, or tampering with conscience, religious
knowledge, though clear as the sun at noon-day, it
must be allowed, can afford *no* peace : nay far, very
far be it from us to try and *give* comfort in such a
case ; as wretchedness is the only hopeful symptom,
and we should hail it as we do the wincing of
the flesh at the touch of the lancet, under suspended animation ; which gives hopes that life is
not quite extinct. And that, while " the whole
body is in darkness from the eye being evil," still
" it is a darkness that may be *felt ;*" and that misery
alone, if no better motive prevails, may drive back
the sufferer to him from whom he has so deeply revolted, and the truth of whose words he so acutely
feels : " Know, therefore, and see, that it is an evil
thing. and bitter, that thou hast forsaken the Lord
thy God ; and that my fear is not in thee, saith the
Lord of Hosts." (Jer. ii. 19.) And painful as the
spectacle is, it is much less so—nay, often a relief
to witness, compared to the awful sight of natural
cheerfulness sustained by a backsliding professor
immersed in the pleasures and business of this life,
" having a name to live whilst he is dead," and saying, " I am rich and increased with goods, and have

need of nothing, and knowing not that he is wretched, and miserable, and poor, and blind, and naked," as a broken and contrite spirit, we know, God will not despise; but a heart divided between two masters can have no acceptance in his sight.

Let it not be alleged, that it is placing religion on a very selfish footing, thus grounding the necessity of it on personal comfort; for as we feel assured that not only can there be no walk with God without it, " for can two walk together except they be agreed?" but no entrance even into the divine life, we press it upon the attention, as the very post from which we must start to begin the journey heavenwards.

And unless religion presents itself with an agreeable aspect to our minds, we cannot expect it will have power sufficient to attract our regard, and win our affections, which are seduced on all sides by the enticing pleasures of the world, that assert their influence over our senses, and require some counteracting influence, fully stronger than theirs, to conquer their ascendency over us. We may indeed gain converts from the ranks of those who are mourning over the withered hopes and blighted joys of earth; but we have no chance of tempting any from its ensnaring amusements, or rendering any superior to *their* force; unless we can insure them, in compensation for their loss of these idle vanities, a real, substantial, and *sensible* good, which will effectually supplant all these lesser objects, and overpower, with its superior sweetness, all these alluring but dangerous sources of gratification. And let the disciple of Christ be well assured, that with the many self-denying sacrifices " of the things which perish in the using," and of those tempers and tastes which are inimical to our progress heavenwards, are given to us joys unspeakable here, and a hope full of immortality hereafter!

How many are wandering from preacher to preacher, and from party to party, seeking rest and finding none, while the elements of peace lie neglected in their own minds : for " Light is sown for the righteous, and joy for the upright in heart." And we must cultivate this seed sown within us, and strewn around us, to fill our bosom with the sheaves of those fruits of the Spirit, which are love, *joy, peace*," &c.

Those who are seeking for their rest in the secondary and subsidiary means of outward ordinances of any kind, in place of having their eye singly directed to God, may obtain a temporary relief from them, but one which only makes them feel more sensibly afterwards, they do not possess the things which they longed for : for they have " committed two evils, they have forsaken the fountain head of living waters, and have hewed out for themselves cisterns, broken cisterns, which can hold no water ;"

and when these are removed, they feel with one of
old, " Ye have taken away my gods, and what have
I more?" For when our eye is double, "our whole
body is full of darkness," and consequently misery ;
" for if *the light* that is in us *be darkness,* how great
is *that* darkness ! "

" I am the light of the world," saith the Lord,
" and he that followeth me shall not walk in darkness, but shall have the light of life :" and, " These
things have I spoken unto you, that in me ye should
have *peace ;*" and, " These things have I spoken unto
you, that your *joy* should be full." If any, then, are
filled instead with anxiety, uncertainty, and distress,
with regard to their soul's interests, they prove to
a demonstration that " they are not following the
Lord fully." Or they are not possessed of his truth :
the distinctive proof of obtaining which, was to be
evidenced by such a strong influence over our feelings, that none who possessed it could remain unconscious of: and by such a powerful effect on our
conduct as to make it observable to every one round
us: " For if we *say* that we have fellowship with him,
and walk in darkness, we lie, and do not the truth :"
for " I am come a light into the world, that whosoever believeth in me should not walk in darkness."

Therefore, " while there be many that say, who
will show us any good?" Lord, lift thou up the light
of thy countenance upon us, should be our prayer ;

and let us follow the directions of the Psalmist, who says, this light put more joy and gladness in his heart, than in the time when their corn, and wine, and oil increased, who sought their joy from other sources. " Stand in awe, and sin not; commune with your own heart in your chamber, and be still ; offer the sacrifice of righteousness, and put your trust in the Lord :" neglect not outward ordinances and means of grace, but lean not on them, look not to them as the *end*, but as the instruments of obtaining for us the end of our salvation, even making Him take up his abode in our hearts, " who is our *Peace !*" And let us form the resolution the pious and learned Joseph Mede advises all to do, " Renounce all kind of peace, till thou hast found the peace of conscience ; discard all joy, till thou feelest the joy of the Holy Ghost : doe this, and there is no calamity so great, but thou maist undergo: no burden so heavy, but thou maist easily bear it : doe this, and thou shalt live in the fear, dye in the favour, and rise in the power of God the Father, and help to make up the heavenly concert, singing with the saints and angels Hallelujah."

CHAPTER II.

BESIDES the grief man is subject to from any of the misfortunes of life, or " the ills flesh is heir to," befalling him; from the distraction which its cares may occasion him, and the discomfort arising from the insecurity of his best enjoyments, and the fleeting nature of them all; it must be evident to every reflecting and observant mind, that there is a yet deeper-seated source of disquietude within his own bosom, which gives him more uneasiness than all the rest put together, and which is often a cause of acute misery to him, in the absence of all these, in a feeling of want, and a sense of mental vacuity, for which this world, richly furnished as it is with means for the supply of his necessities, and with everything that can minister to the gratification of his tastes, affords him no adequate provision, and which his own efforts have as utterly failed in supplying, as they have in ascertaining the cause by the efforts of his own understanding.

Every other species of uneasiness may be traced up to its source : and to the loss of friends, property, health, &c., we may charge home the blame of the grief which oppresses us : but this unassignable one, which has its roots in the hidden and inaccessible regions of the soul, as entirely defies our attempts at its relief, as it does our endeavours at investigation into its cause. And whilst it is an evil under which ancient and modern minds have alike groaned, it has as much baffled the enlightened minds of the present day, as it did those of the most learned sages of the past ! Does it not indeed seem strange, that when all inferior animals have a provision given them, quite adequate to the extent of their wants and capacities of enjoyment, that man, the noblest of them all, should be left apparently destitute of one suitable for his highest faculties? and which, left unappeased, pours disrelish upon all inferior enjoyments within his reach : and that, except by descending from the lofty pedestal on which nature has placed him, and lowering the high powers and aspirings of his mind to a level with that of the beasts which perish, confining himself solely to the exercise of those appetites and passions which he shares in common with them; preying, for instance, upon the weaker of *their* species, or waging war upon his own, or plunging into sensuality, experiencing, meanwhile, the worm of dissatisfaction and disgust at his

heart's core,—he cannot find room for the exercise of
his powers, or food for the cravings of his nature.
And even when he ascends into the purer atmosphere of intellectual pursuits, whence is it that he
finds them even more signally fail in realising his
expectations? One acquirement after another fail-
ing to satisfy his desires, and only leaving a more
aching void than before, the bitterness of disappointment being enhanced from *their* having approached more nearly to the fulfilment of his hopes.
St. Augustine has given us a reason, which, as far
as it goes, is satisfactory : " Thou hast made us for
thyself, and our soul is restless until it resteth in
thee," says he, appealing to his Maker. " My heart
and my flesh crieth out for the living God,'' is the feeling of the soul, that, like the dove sent out of the ark,
has flitted over the unquiet ocean of life, and, finding no place of repose, longs for a resting-place " in
the bosom of her Father and her God."

But whence is it, then, that when the soul feels
these intense longings after a higher and fuller bliss
than earth can afford, and which it is persuaded that
nothing but proximity to its Maker can bestow, that
when it flees thither, as to " the haven where it
would be," it is incapable of reaching it, or returns
as if repulsed, and when the hour arrives for it to
draw near to God, it is oppressed with such a deep-
felt sense of inability for the holy exercise, that, like

the flying-fish out of water, it is unable to sustain
its flight, but sinks immediately into the grosser ele-
ment of the flesh, though attracted by an unseen
magnet above, and repelled from below by the unsatisfactory nature of all earth's enjoyments? Nay,
that not only an inability, but a positive repugnance
to the task is felt by all who cannot, like the forma-
list, rest contented with mere lip-service, but seek
to worship the Father of their spirits in spirit and
in truth ; who are too painfully conscious, that whilst
in all other occupations in which they engage, that
present any object of interest, they have but to *follow* nature in pursuing it, in this they must *force*
nature to accomplish it, though it is one undeniably
of more importance to us than any other, including
both the interests of time and eternity; for whenever the opportunity of solitary intercourse with
their Maker arrives, unlike the fabled waters of old,
that shrank back from the lips of Tantalus, our
minds shrink back from the living waters which flow
to our lips. If we try to account for this, by affirming that this repugnance is felt only by those whose
minds are alienated from God by the wickedness that
is in them, and whose consciences, testifying thus
against them, recoil from the all-searching eye of
Heaven,—we have but to watch the feelings of a
little child, unsoiled yet by any deadly sin, and un-
regenerated by the Spirit of God ; and, however we

may try to convince it, it is a good thing to draw
nigh to God, that it has no cause to fear him, and
every reason to love and praise him, a remnant of
the old Adam in his breast speaks a truer language
to him than all our reasonings, and the wandering
eye, the restless body, the distracted attention, will
convince us " the way of man is not in him." It is
neither according to his nature, nor agreeable to his
feelings, to hold converse with his God.   And how
can we account for the fact, that in all recorded
manifestations of the Deity, in whatever form he
has been pleased to appear to man, in place of that
elation of mind, that exuberance of joy, we should
expect upon such an occasion, man sinks to the
earth, as if crushed beneath the weight of the very
glory he had invoked perhaps to behold. And " now
mine eye seeth thee; wherefore I abhor myself,
and repent in dust and ashes,'' bursts from his lips.
That the wicked, who drink in iniquity like water,
should cry out, " Depart from us, for we desire not
the knowledge of thy ways," can excite no surprise :
but that the excellent of the earth should have been
thus always overwhelmed, demands explanation.
That they who have their portion in this life, and
who, from the ignorance that is in them, and the
degradation to which their corrupt habits have sunk
them, should be contented to feed on husks fit only
for the swine to eat, and should feel none of this

mental uneasiness and vacuity of soul, is no explanation why minds of a superior class, attempting, apparently, more perfectly to fulfil the high behests of their being, should be left destitute of the power of doing so, and without a provision sufficient to its accomplishment.

But what we have at present in view, is not merely to state that these things are so, which is a truth so palpably evident to men's senses that few will deny it; but to inquire and explain the reason *why* they are so, in dependence on the assistance of God.

It was not always thus with man! Scripture informs us, which is the only authority entitled or enabled to explain the truth to us, the reversed position man now occupies in the scale of creation is very different from that in which he was originally installed, and for which he was originally intended, till his own act and deed displaced him from it. This avowed defect in his nature to fulfil the purposes of his high destiny, is very opposite to that state of healthful vigour and moral aptitude for their performance, with which he was plentifully endued, when, placed at the head of creation, he stood as the high priest of nature, to offer up her spiritual sacrifices of praise and prayer to the Almighty, and audibly to interpret her dumb voice of gratitude to him for all his mercies and goodness:

" The monarch of all he surveyed,
    And lord of the fowl and the brute."—Cowper.

which all owned his sway, by passing under his hand,
in token of subjection, each to receive from his lips
its appropriate name—he himself yet, equally with
the meanest of them, a pensioner of the Divine
bounty, yielded his willing tribute of thanks and
praise to him, at whose hands he held, and to whose
goodness he must stand indebted for the preservation of all he possessed. Nor must we attach the
idea of degradation to dependence or servility to
homage we are proud to do, from seeing it, in the
present morbid state of human feelings and disor-
ganized state of human society, with imperious
and oppressive tempers on the one hand, and the
unsubdued spirit of pride on the other—a burden
onerous to bear, and a spectacle painful to witness.
For, even in this present lamentable state of things,
there are some bright exceptions to them, that may
enable us to form an idea what it must have been under happier circumstances, when man was in a situation to call forth the exercise of his best affections,
and before he had disqualified himself for all his
duties and enjoyments. A devoted sister, an attached wife, feels it to be anything but a mortification to lean upon the manly arm of the stronger
sex for support, fly to them for assistance, and look

up to their superior intellect for advice and information : inequality of power, by engendering dependence in the one, and giving the sense of guardian-
ship in the other, only cementing thus, and
sweetening more, the tie that binds them. When
man was placed in paradise with a mind yet in a
state of unsullied purity, with bodily powers in
unimpaired strength, and with every affection
flowing in its right channel; surrounded by such
marks of the divine wisdom and majesty as must have
filled his soul with the sublimest ideas of his Maker,
and receiving every hour such proofs of God's
goodness and generosity as were calculated to
awaken and secure every feeling of gratitude and
attachment to him, and admitted to an intercourse
with him of the most intimate and endearing kind,
the most ennobling to his nature and the most exalting to his feelings we can conceive, and endued
with the power of fully estimating it,—he was in
no want of an object worthy of engrossing the
attention of an immortal being, or of satisfying the
best and purest feelings of his heart.

Those who deem it a privilege to become acquainted with such as are eminent for excellence, or
celebrated for talent or acquirements, or who consider it a mark of favour and distinction to be admitted into the presence-chamber of the kings and
great men of the earth, may be able to form an esti-

mate of what it must have been to have had free
access to the presence of the Wonderful, the Coun-
sellor, the Ancient of days, the King of kings and
Lord of lords! No wonder that the soul that had
ever entertained such a guest, should refuse to be
comforted under the loss of his presence! No
wonder that the mind that had thus fed on angels'
food, should be unable to feel contented under any
meaner provision.

Restricted but by one prohibition, " Of every
tree of the garden thou mayest freely eat, but of
the tree of knowledge of good and evil, thou shalt
not eat of it: for in the day that thou eatest thereof
thou shalt surely die," (Gen. ii.) he, as we all too
well know, found this one small test of his obedience too great; he was not proof against the wiles
of the devil, nor prepared for the weakness of his
own heart, but at the instigation of his wife, who
had already fallen into the snare of the tempter, he
took of the tree, and did eat thereof; in a moment,
what fatal consequences ensued !

> " 'Twas but one little drop of sin
>   We saw this morning enter in,
> And now, at even-tide, the world is drowned !"
>   KEBLE.

In place of those feelings of joy and confidence
with which he must hitherto have hailed the voice
of his great Creator and Benefactor, when he drew

near in the cool of the evening to commune with
him, he heard that voice, and ran to hide himself
among the trees of the garden. Hide himself!
from whom? From "Him who was his life, and
the length of his days!" "Can any hide himself in
secret places that *I* cannot see them?" saith He
whose eyes are in every place, beholding the evil
and the good. But why does he hide himself?
Love seeks no concealment; innocence needs no
screen. When asked the reason of his conduct by
God, he answers, "I was afraid." Awful truth,
which has convulsed the whole of nature ever since!
" Whither shall I flee from thy presence?" being the
sensation of the first sinner, as it shall be that of
the last, when he "calls upon the rocks to fall on
him, and the hills to cover him from the face of
God and the Lamb."

What a contrast does Adam now present!

> " If thou be'st he !—but oh! how fallen, how chang'd,
> From him who, in the happy realms of light,
> Cloth'd in transcendent brightness !"—MILTON.

had been so lately pronounced by his God "very
good." "How is the gold become dim—how is the
most fine gold changed! the crown has fallen from
his head, for he has sinned." That fear of the
divine vengeance formed one part of his mind's
suffering, and was one cause of the sudden change

D

in his feelings, there can be no doubt ; but that it
formed but one ingredient in the bitter cup he had
taken into his hand to drink, few will question, if
they have ever felt a desire to stand high in the
good opinion of a friend every way worthy of
their esteem, and possessing their fondest affection ;
and who have ever committed an act that would
tend to lower them in their regard, and might lead
them to forfeit their affection; or who has ever seen
one that had been loaded with favours by a kind
and generous person, who had repaid all with the
basest ingratitude, brought suddenly into contact
with their injured benefactor ; or who has ever
heard the shriek of distress of a child fondly loved by
its parents, and tenderly loving in return, dragged by
its nurse into their presence, to have a fault ex-
posed,—have had some samples of the complicated
emotion of remorse, fear and shame, wounded pride
and self-accusation, which must have shaken the
frame of our first father, when he heard the voice
of God saying, " Where art thou ?" All the remembered proofs of the love of that gracious Being he
had so wantonly offended, would now be as so many
daggers to his heart ; all the gifts of his bounty
surrounding him, as so many sparks of fire in his
eyes, and with the painful burden of past recollec-
tions would be mingled also fearful anticipations of
future punishment, imagination conjuring up, proba-

bly, harrowing ideas of the meaning of that mysterious threat impending over him, " In the day that
thou eatest thereof thou shalt surely die.   Such a
total and instantaneous change in the feelings and
aspect of the mind has no parallel in nature, no
likeness wherewith we can liken it to, save that
of which it was not merely the type, but the spiritual realization, death ; when the form that we
beheld in the morning, in the bloom of youth and
beauty, is stretched before us at evening a lifeless corpse.   For this was, indeed, that " dying
thou shalt die," which was to take place *in the day*
man transgressed God's command, that change *in
the mind* which instantaneously was the consequence
of his so doing; and was the initial fulfilment
and spiritual antepast of that fuller consummation of
the sentence which was not to take place till dust
returned to its kindred dust, out of which it had
been taken.   What the light is to the natural world,
God is to the spiritual; and as we can easily conceive
what sad consequences would ensue to the animal
and vegetable world, which hung dependent on its
cheering and fructifying beams for existence, were
that bright and glorious luminary the sun to be
withdrawn ; we may, from analogy, imagine what
must have been the state of utter desolation and
bereavement of the soul, when " He, in whom
it lived and moved and had its being," was, by the

interposition of the body of sin and death eclipsed,
and the light of his countenance shone no more
upon it.   Here, then, we have, from the pen of inspiration, a solution of the problem which has
baffled the intellects of man at its highest pitch of
cultivation in ancient days, and still remains one
insoluble to every mind at the present day, that
does not seek for its key in the Holy Scriptures,
why man is displaced from that high post he
seemed destined to fill in the creation of God, and
occupies a much lower one than nature evidently
ever intended him for ; in which his every faculty is
cramped, and his every power insufficient for the
exercises in which it is his duty and his interest to
engage, while yet he retains such a thirst after
purer and higher sources of gratification than earth
can ever afford, as betrays the link which bound
him to his first parent, and dragged him down with
him from his high elevation to this low standing
place in the world.   As all mankind were included
in Adam, we have every reason to suppose that
had he kept his first estate, they too would
have entered upon his fair heritages, and come
into the world heirs of all the blessings he enjoyed ; consequently all were involved in his disgrace, and came into it stripped of all these goodly
possessions which he had by transgression for feited,
and, "begotten after *his* likeness" in mind and cir-

cumstances, exiled from paradise, and the sword
of the divine wrath flashing in their eyes, in place
of God's voice of peace and love sounding in their
ears, as it had done to Adam before he fell : and
this exclusion from the divine presence exists with
every man in his natural state, who has not availed
himself of the title to restoration, redemption has
bestowed upon him. And though no fiery sword
addresses itself to our senses, yet the intuitive consciousness of it remains in every unrenewed bosom.
And this painful sense of estrangement from our
Maker, the author and end of our existence, is felt
by many minds, long before our alienation from
him by reason of sin is discovered ; and it is to be
regretted that persons of this description are not
oftener addressed as a separate class by preachers,
since it forms a barrier as impassable between their
souls and God, as that which our iniquities have
raised up, and our sins have builded. Strong denunciations against gross and convicted sinners, fly
harmlessly over *their* heads, who need an arrow
winged with a much more delicate feather to bring
home to their conscience the fact that they belong
to that class at all, and who require to be taught
that not only the deliberate violater of God's law,
but the most decent and comparatively upright
living man amongst us, " Except he be born again,
he cannot see the kingdom of God." Such igno-

rance prevails both on the subject of the immaculate
purity and the inaccessible holiness of the divine
nature, before whom the highest cherubim veil
their faces with their wings, and cry " Holy, holy,
holy, Lord God of Sabaoth," and before every manifestation of whose presence below, the holiest saints
have ever fallen to the earth as dead men : and
such false ideas are entertained of the inherent dignity and excellency of human nature, and so little
is understood of the extent of men's degeneracy
and deterioration by the fall, that the distance
which exists between us, worms of the dust, and an
unapproachably holy God, is so little known, that
the instinctive sense of it which conscience retains,
is unintelligible to many, who are conscious of its
movements, and yet have a very indistinct apprehension of the cause which occasions it. So that
many, whose feet are stumbling on the dark mountains of error on this subject, " seeking after
God, if haply they might feel after and find him,"
crying, " O that I knew *where* I might find him,
that I might come even to his seat !" were God to
grant them their request, and the thing that they
long for ;" and were one ray of the brightness of his
presence to fall upon them, would cry out, " Depart
from me, for I am a sinful man, O Lord !" The
spirituality of God's law, too, and the heart-searching length it goes, is so little understood by most

men, as such glosses have been put upon its inter-
pretation; and men are so accustomed to judge of
it after the manner in which they see human laws
administered; and also to take the low standard of
virtue that prevails below, as an estimate of what prevails with God, that it is necessary to explain this
more fully, before we can convince every man that,
besides the exclusion from the presence of his Maker
the *fall* has occasioned, each man has himself given a
cause for this exclusion by his own individual sins—
for, alas! there is no human conscience that has
reason to shrink back from the presence of God, *only*
because our first Father has deprived us all of our
natural right to draw near him as innocent persons;
but every one has too much reason to do so on its
own account, did it know what God is, and what sin
is in his eyes!

Man's law, which reaches only to the hearing of
the ear and the seeing of the eye, can take cogni-
zance but of the *outward* act of disobedience; consequently, however appearances are against a man,
unless suspicion amounts to proof, the law cannot
touch him, he must go free. But God's law goes a
length no *human* code ever reached; nay, if it tried
to do so, must utterly fail of power to carry it into
effect: transgression against *it* extends to the very
thoughts, intentions, and inclinations to sin, secretly
indulged in or purposed by the soul; and He who

"does *not* judge after the seeing of the eye and the hearing of the ear," but who searcheth the *hearts* to give unto every man according to what its secrets disclose, holds that man guilty of a breach of his law who has encouraged the sinful motion, or planned the wicked deed, though he has never had the opportunity to carry it into action.

Man, too, can only exact outward obedience to his commands, and insist upon compliance with the letter of his instructions, and can take no exception at the spirit in which they are performed—but God does not rest satisfied here : the mere act, in his sight, is as nothing compared to the motive which stimulates and the spirit which actuates us ; and whilst a cup of cold water even, "given in his name," He assures us shall in nowise lose its reward, the most costly offerings without it are worthless.

Men, too, now take great liberties with God's law, so as to make it a burden very light to their conscience, and a yoke very easy to their neck ; and were the infraction of it as small a matter in the eye of *God* as it is in *their* sight, few would have any great apprehension at hearing "they shall all stand before the judgment seat of God !" They have made it a very serious thing, the breach of such commandments as affect the peace and well-being of society, and touch the bond between man and man, but think it a thing of very little moment, comparatively, to transgress such as offend against *God only*. But He who framed the law, and will execute it in the same spirit of righteousness in which it is framed, will make no such exception ; for He that said, Do not commit adultery, said also, Do not kill. Now if thou commit no adultery, yet if thou kill, thou art become a transgressor of the law," equally with him who has transgressed it in another respect ; and the swearer and the sabbath-breaker will find themselves, at the last grand day of assize, ranged in the same class, and subject alike to the indignation and punishment of God, though the laws of man here had visited the sin of the first with severe vengeance, whilst it had let the latter go wholly unpunished. They, too, in their wisdom, have established a wide difference between *the sex* of such as offend against God: and *a man* may hold up his head all the higher in human society, perhaps, who has broken the seventh commandment, whilst *a woman* is, and deservedly, banished from the circles of the virtuous, when she has forfeited her title to their society ; but these distinctions which prevail below, will vanish when we appear before Him with whom "all souls are equal," and with whom there is in Christ Jesus neither Greek nor Jew, neither bond nor free, *neither male nor female ;*" but the judgment of God is according to truth to every *soul* of man that doeth evil ; for there is no respect of per-

sons with God. Many, too, are in such ignorance
as to the wide difference which subsists between
this present dispensation under which we live, and
the past under the Mosaic law, that because sentence
against an evil work is not executed as it was then,
when God slew in one day twenty-three thousand
(1 Cor. x. 8) souls, for a sin now daily committed with
impunity, apparently, by thousands, and when deeds
of wickedness rise up in His ears with a cry as loud
as that which drew down fire and brimstone upon
the cities of the plain, and called down rain from
heaven to wash away the wickedness of a world by
destroying all its population except eight persons,
they think God's holy hatred against sin must be
abated, or his laws against it changed.   Not understanding, that at that time God, by a system of temporal punishments and rewards, was instructing
man in the essential holiness of his character, and
in the horrible nature of sin, " the thing which his
soul hateth," by marking the offender on the spot,
and making the punishment of the offence strike a
just dread of sin, and fear of the consequences of it,
into every human bosom ; but that we are living
under a totally different dispensation in a day of
grace, during which judgment is temporarily suspended, and God is not " entering into judgment
with any man," nor dealing with any according to
his iniquities ;" but having, as it were, shown out to

the utmost his indignation against sin, and his abhorrence of it, in allowing his dear Son to suffer
death upon the cross for us men, and for us miserable sinners, he is no longer under the necessity,
if we may so speak, of thus daily testifying to his
sense of its wickedness, and the extent of his wrath
against it, by his immediate visitations upon all transgressors of his law ; but having retired now behind
the cloud for a season, letting "mercy rejoice
against judgment, and grace abound over sin," if so
be the *goodness* of God may lead men to repentance ;" and "having sent his Son to bless us in
turning away every one of us from our iniquities ;"
He is, in much mercy, waiting to see its effect upon
us,—" not imputing to any man his trespasses," and
so not dealing with him as a transgressor, but has
committed to his church the ministry of *reconciliation*, commanding them to announce to all men the
glad tidings of great joy, that he is not willing that
any should perish, but that the wicked should turn
from the evil of their way and live ; and except when
He steps out of his place occasionally to visit the sin
of some flagrant offender with punishment upon the
spot, or pour His judgments upon a nation, that the
inhabitants of the earth may learn righteousness by
their fate,—having now fully explained to all men
the principles of his government, and the rule of his
judgments, He leaves them to draw their own in-

ferences as to their own fate, and as to that of
others, from this, and bids them walk *by faith* in his
word, "that it shall be well with the righteous, for
he shall eat the fruit of his ways, and ill to the sinner, for the reward of his hands shall be given him;"
and, not judging by the sight of their eyes, under the
present dispensation of grace, when good and evil are
happening alike to all. But let none mistake this merciful forbearance of God for a change in his feelings
towards the sin, or of his ultimate intentions as to
the fate of the impenitent sinner. " The Lord our
Lord is *one Lord.*" "I am the Lord, *I change not,*"
is his declaration; and though He for a time, and
with a most gracious purpose to us, has changed
the mode of his proceeding with us, his hatred
against sin is not altered, nor are his laws against it
repealed, although suspended in operation. Therefore, if any, presuming upon His present long-suffering mercy, and long-sparing patience, think that
he will never have the heart to cast any away
from his presence at his coming, they will find
out, alas! too late, that though they *could* not extend their ideas of the pitifulness of his mercy too
far now, in this "day of grace," when, "like as a
father pitieth his children, even so the Lord pitieth
them that fear him," they were not entitled to
transfer these feelings to the "day of judgment,"
when He who now stands with the golden sceptre of

mercy in his hand stretched out, waiting to be
gracious, saying, " Come unto me," shall appear
with the sharp two-edged sword proceeding out of
his mouth, to "smite the earth with the rod of his
mouth—and with the breath of his lips to slay the
wicked :" and He who says now, as our Saviour, I
came not to judge the world, but to save it, " *shall*
come to be our judge ," " for God hath appointed a
day in which he shall judge the world in righteousness *by that man* whom he hath ordained.'' Acts
xviii. 31.

Who, then, that takes this solemn and awful view
of himself, thus shown him by God's word, and hears
what the holiness of that God is, " who requireth
truth in the inward parts," and " sets our secret sins
in the light of his countenance,"—"in whose sight
the very heavens are not clean, and who chargeth
even his angels with folly ; behold even to the moon,
and it shineth not, and the stars are not pure in his
sight ; how much more man that is a worm, and the
son of man, which is as a worm ;" and who that sees
what a length the heart-searching law of God goes,
and finds that he that breaketh *one* of his commandments is guilty of *all*; (James ii. 10 ;) forhe as effectually breaks that chain which bound his soul to
heaven, by breaking *one* link, as by breaking a
dozen : for though more may increase his guilt, yet
one effects his ruin ;—who, I say, that takes all this

into consideration, will dare to say, " I have made
my heart pure, I am clean from mine iniquity," and
venture ever to stand before God on the ground of
innocence, or to challenge his regard on the score
of spotless purity? Nay, strange and paradoxical
as it may appear, those that we should imagine
were most likely to fall into this error, from their
ever " exercising themselves to have a conscience
void of offence towards God and towards man," are
always the least liable to do so, as their thus " laying judgment so constantly to the line," and righteousness to the plummet of God's law, makes
them so conscious of the smallest obliquity
from the straight rule of right, that *they* are
too sensible of their hourly aberrations from the
path of duty ever to be found in the posture of
the pharisee, " God, I thank thee that I am not
as other men are," but ever in that of the pub-
lican, " God be merciful to me a sinner." Watchfulness and self-examination will bring home to all
hearts the truth of those words, " Who can bring a
clean thing out of an unclean? No, not one." " Can
the Ethiopian change his skin, or the leopard his
spots? then may you do good who have been accustomed to do evil." And any who go about
to establish their own righteousness, and will not
submit to the righteousness of God, even the righteousness which is of faith, will be taught, like one of

old, " Though I wash myself in srow-water, and make myself ever so clean, yet shalt thou plunge me in the ditch, so that my own clothes shall abhor me," by being allowed such a sight of the evil of his nature as to make him own, if I justify myself, my own mouth shall condemn me ; if I say I am perfect, it shall prove me perverse. And if he of whom God has recorded, " there was none like him on the earth, a perfect and an upright man, one that feared God and eschewed evil," made *this* avowal, surely there is no man on earth now who would venture to say less than " Enter not into judgment with thy servant, O Lord, for in thy sight shall *no man living be justified !* "

Thus while everything around a man indicates to him he is in a fallen world, and confirms the truth of God's word, that " this is not his rest, for it is polluted," the very ground he treads on being cursed for his sake, and brings forth only thorns and thistles, till the sweat of his brow wrings from it more suitable nutriment for his wants ; the beasts of the field having revolted from under his hand, as he has from under the authority of his Maker, everything within him, too, testifies to the truth, that though God made man upright," he has defaced the divine image in which he was created, so much, that he needs to be renewed ere he can recover the noble lineaments he has lost. His body is a prey to

weakness, disease, and decay, and the subject of
death, which all his life long, like the sword of
Damocles, hangs as if suspended over him by a single
hair—the poisoner of all his present enjoyments,
and the fruitful source of his disquietude regarding
the future.   His mind is yet in a worse condition ;
its peace may be either wrecked by grief and care,
or so destroyed by the evil passions within his own
breast, or the sour and malignant tempers of those
around him, as to make "his life a weariness to
him."   The powers with which he is endowed, he
feels, are disabled for their highest exercises, and
yet too noble in their origin to be satisfactorily employed in meaner occupations ; and however he may
" labour in the fire for very vanity" to rear a
monument worthy of the natural gifts conferred
on him, or the ambitious feelings of his mind, still,
whatever splendid trophies he may raise to com-
memorate the skill and talent of the contriver, all
these grand achievements can accompany him only
to the tomb ; they may be heaped up at its outside,
but none of them can pass through the dark portals
of the grave with him.   " As he came forth of his
mother's womb, naked shall he return, to go as he
came, and shall take nothing of his labour which he
may carry away in his hand ; in all points as he came,
so shall he go.   And what profit hath he that hath
laboured for the wind ? for how dieth the wise man ?

even as the fool! (Eccles. v. 15.) And even if looking on the works his hands had wrought, and behold there was no profit under the sun, he takes refuge in more intellectual employments. Though he turn himself to behold Wisdom, and his heart has great experience of wisdom and knowledge, and though he can speak of trees from the cedar tree that is in Lebanon even unto the hyssop that springeth out of the wall, and of beasts, and of fowls, and of creeping things, and of fishes; he will find that this also is vexation of spirit, for in much wisdom is much grief, and he that increaseth knowledge increaseth sorrow, and the sum of the whole matter is vanity of vanities, all is vanity! It is no contradiction of this statement to say, that many dissent from this account of things, and declare that they find the pursuits of literature, science, and the arts, afford them abundant present enjoyment, and sufficient food for future expectation. As the moment of illusion, when hope is on the horizon, is not the moment it can be *felt*, nor will any almost, learn from any experience but their own, that " though they may plant pleasant plants, and may set strange slips; in the day they shall make their plant to grow, and in the morning shall make their seed to flourish ; but the harvest shall be a heap in the day of grief and of desperate sorrow." (Isa. xvii. 10, 11.) And all these evils in man's lot,

E

we have now seen, are to be traced up, not only to
the sin of our first father, " who brought death into
the world and all our woe," but are also to be brought
home and laid at each man's own door ; for so far
from any one having lessened the barrier which Adam
raised, and done anything to remove the cause of
exclusion from the Divine presence, every man
has added his " many offences" (Rom. v. 16) to the
one sin by which death entered into the world, and
has too good reason to cry out on his own account,
" O wretched man that I am ! who shall deliver me
from the body of this death ?"

CHAPTER III.

But it would be doing a very small service to prove that it is a fact that "man is very far gone from original righteousness," and merely to explain the cause of their misfortunes, unless at the same time we could point out a remedy for the evil, by showing how the barrier which man's sins had raised between him and his Maker has been removed, and the ample means for his recovery which has been provided. To bid a man be at ease and enjoy all the blessings of life around him, whilst he knew that the sentence against him as a sinner remained unrepealed, and whilst unforgiven sin rankled in his breast, would be like bidding the wounded man lie still and at his ease, when we had bathed his wound with an anodyne, and left the shaft sticking in it, or exhorting the good man of the house to be happy, and enjoy all the comforts of

E 2

his fireside, when he knew that the robber and the murderer were concealed on his premises, to rise up at midnight for his destruction. No; the cry, " I have sinned, O thou Preserver of man, what shall I do? is not so easily silenced; and if, like blind Bartimeus, we are urged to hold our peace by some who have healed our wounds slightly, " saying, peace, peace, when there was no peace," we shall cry so much the more, " Have mercy on me !" As the wound cannot heal round a thorn, no more can that which sin has inflicted on the heart be cured, till it has been probed by self-examination, discovered by confession, and the barbed arrow extracted by the hand of the good Physician of souls, who alone can restore ease to the mind by saying, " Thy sins are forgiven thee; go in peace." Sin, inwardly festering in the soul, forbids the possibility of peace; and even though we may for a time succeed in lulling the sense of it asleep, or in driving away the remembrance of it, and may say, " Soul, take thine ease, eat, drink, and be merry," " be sure your sin shall find you out;" it shall wake that will bite you; will glare upon you in your hour of solitary retirement, or rise up suddenly before you at the social board, like Banquo's ghost; will unnerve the powers of your mind, and unstring the sinews of your body. If the Protestant religion does not give *this* peace, it gives us less than the Jew's reli-

gion did, which unquestionably enabled its possessor
to taste "the blessedness of those whose iniquities were forgiven, and their sin covered;" (Ps.
xxxii.;) and less than the apostate Romish church
undertakes to give her disciples, who permits them
to purchase it with the gold which perisheth, or to
obtain it by meritorious service; if our religion,
then, gave us not, at least as much as the former
was able to give, and the latter pretends to give her
children, we should be tempted to renounce Christianity and return to the Jewish persuasion, or to
accept of Rome's fictitious counterfeit,* as even
the amount of the one, or the unsubstantial idea of
the other, would, to weak minds, be better than none
at all! But, "blessed be the God and Father of
our Lord Jesus Christ, who hath blessed us with all

---

* Indeed we have every reason to believe that for the relief
of anxiety on this subject, and from impatience under the discomfort which the uncertainty men's minds are involved in by
the present style of preaching, (which seems more intended to
awaken men to a sense of want than a knowledge of the source
whence all these wants are supplied,) many have taken refuge
in Romanism, and many would do so were they not deterred by
the fresh troubles in which such a step plunges them; indo-
lence and timidity alone preserving them members of the Protestant body, while their minds pant after what they erroneously
conceive Catholicism alone can bestow on them, peace of mind
arising from a sense of the forgiveness of their sins and restoration to the favour of God.

spiritual blessings in Christ Jesus," we are not
driven to either of these miserable expedients to
obtain this "pearl of great price," peace of mind,
through the pardon of our sins, which was only
dimly revealed to the Jews, in its dark cabinet of
type and figure, and which Rome stole from the
world in all its disclosed and refulgent lustre in the
Gospel, and replaced with the baubles of human
corruptions and inventions; but we, in this our day,
may know the things that belong to our peace, with
no such dreadful sacrifices, having a ground of hope
" upon the best and surest foundations," containing
all that the most guilty require for their cleansing,
all that the most helpless stand in need of for their
support, and the most wretched could desire, to
alleviate their distress, so placed within the reach
of every creature that breathes, that he who does
not know " the exceeding riches of God's grace, in
" His kindness towards us, through Christ Jesus,"
and consequently is not " rejoicing with a joy unspeakable and a hope full of immortality," is living
below his privileges, and below that state of peace
and joy in believing, his God has provided for him;
and is thus depriving himself of his due heritage,
and robbing God of the glory due to his most holy
name, who has appointed so full a provision for his
edification and comfort. Yes—without making
light of sin, as some well-meaning writers do, to

give relief to the suffering conscience, without lowering the high standard of God's most holy law to our necessities, in despair that we could ever reach its requirements ; without detracting from the holy character of Him with whom we have do, " making Him such a one as ourselves," lest the knowledge of Him *as He is* should annihilate us ; without trying to cloak and hide our sins from his sight, and " make the best of ourselves" as a late writer advises, but looking our sin in the face, in all its exceeding sinfulness, regarding God in his true light as the hater and avenger of it, and owning our just desert of the extremest punishment his law denounces against transgressors ; we, on grounds which can stand the test of the most searching examination by the light of God's word, the most careful scrutiny of our own anxious misgivings, and the most earnest investigation of every honest mind that asks us for " a reason of the hope that is in us," possess a foundation of peace and comfort we can challenge the whole world to equal in extent, and defy its utmost efforts and power to shake. " For I am persuaded," says one who had long possessed it, and well knew its value, " that neither life, nor death, nor angels, nor principalities, nor powers, nor things present, nor things to come, nor height, nor depth, nor any other creature, shall be able to separate us from the love of God which is in Christ Jesus."

" Acquaint thyself with God, then, and be at peace,"
is the Scripture's invitation and promise : and we
have only to examine it, to ascertain it has given
us no pledge it is unable to redeem to the uttermost
extent of our expectations.

We should, perhaps, be better able to bear the
full effulgence of " the glory of God in the face of
Jesus Christ," which bursts upon us in the Gospel,
if we were to begin by examining and analysing,
first, some of those separate rays which singly
visited the church under the Old Testament dispensation, before " the Sun of Righteousness had
arisen with healing under its wings," above the
spiritual horizon ; and which, " like the morning
spread upon the mountains," " had, as it were, no
glory, by reason of the glory which excelleth ;" and
then proceed to gather up the scattered particles of
light, and present them in their one grand whole,
" Jesus Christ and him crucified," to whom all the
prophets and the law bore witness, and to which all
the events in the history of God's chosen and typical people had a reference ; till we find the opening
leaves of type and prophecy unfold by degrees,
and expand into the full revealed glory " of the
redemption of the world by our Lord Jesus Christ :"
and in comparing the indistinct intimations they
convey, and the dim information they afford to the
mind, of " the revelation of the mystery, which had

been hid in God in former generations, but was now
made known to the church," we may better understand our present privileges, and our Lord's expressive words, " Blessed are your eyes, for they see,
and'your ears, for they hear ; for I say unto you, that
many prophets and righteous men desired to see the
things that ye see, and saw them not, and to hear
the words that ye hear, and heard them not."
These rays of light are spread over such an extent
of surface, and amplified by such a variety of illus-
tration, that it will only be possible, in a brief work
like this, to select a few of the most striking and
important of them : let us, then, open our Bible
at the first chapters of Leviticus, and carefully
observe what a Jew, convicted of sin, and so shut
out from the services of the sanctuary and the
society of God's people, was ordered to do under the
Mosaic economy, to obtain forgiveness, peace of
conscience, restoration to all his forfeited privileges,
besides averting all those penal inflictions which
were brought upon the sinner then by an infraction
of God's commandments. He is desired to bring
an animal of a particular kind, appointed by the
law, expressly selected to denote, by its freedom
from a ferocious nature and unoffending habits, its
fitness for the purpose; and upon the head of an
animal thus emblematic of innocence and useful-
ness he was commanded " to lay his hands," " con-

fessing over it his sins," and was then to kill it
"before the Lord ;" and, after certain ceremonies
and distribution of the parts, the priest officiating
was to burn the flesh in the fire ; and he was then
told " it was accepted for him," to make an *atonement* for him, and that in consequence his sin was
forgiven him. (4th and 5th chapters.) Thus, by
an impressive and significant ceremony, was he
taught the meaning of the mysterious clause in the
gracious attributes of the Almighty vouchsafed to
Moses, that though " he was a God merciful and
gracious, long-suffering, abundant in goodness and
truth : keeping mercy for thousands, forgiving iniquity, transgression, and sin, yet will by no means
clear the guilty," (Exod· xxxiv. 11,) (the insertion of
which seemed to nullify all the rest, and to deprive the sinner of the benefit of them ;) for here
they see that " He had given them the blood of
these victims, to make an atonement for their souls ;"
(Levit. xvii. 11;) which they might understand faintly
by seeing another suffer in their stead ; and their
guilt thus figuratively transferred to another head,
guiltless of their crime, yet accepted by God in
their place, and suffering the death on their account
they had deserved ; the burning of whose flesh in the
fire, too, set forth before their eyes, in a lively and striking manner, the fire which never should be quenched,
that must have been their portion had they died un-

pardoned, "for after death comes the judgment,"
had not God provided a substitute, and had not One,
able and willing to undertake the office, said, "Deliver from going down into the pit, for I have found a
ransom for him," and their forgiveness procured for
them by the divine interposition and mercy, which
had rescued them from irretrievable ruin, showed
them sin pardoned indeed, but not unavenged—forgiven but not unexpiated, but their salvation purchased at the cost of another's blood, which was
poured on the earth for their salvation; and on
whose head the blow they had deserved had fallen,
which otherwise would have sunk their soul into the
pit of perdition. Forgiveness obtained by such
means, must have given them an awful idea of the
nature of sin which could only be expiated by such
a sacrifice, and would tend to make them think anything but lightly of the transgression of a law which
demanded such a reparation for its breach; so that
their thankfulness for the pardon must have been
mingled with a deep sense of humiliation at observing the means used for their absolution, and much
self-abhorrence and self-loathing of the sin which
required such a process for its cleansing. It must,
too, have solemnised their minds, and filled them
with a holy awe of that blessed Being who could
only be approached by sinful man through such a
blood-stained way, and propitiated by such offerings

as these : a keen perception of which forced a Jew
to cry out, " There is forgiveness with thee, that
thou mayest be feared." (Ps. cxxx.) There is forgiveness even with thee, who wilt "by no means clear
the guilty ;" but ah! in what a way! how different
from the mercy which man meets with below, which
is often no more than a weak incapacity to punish,
or disinclination to preserve the integrity of justice,
arising from either sympathy with the sin, or ignorance of its moral turpitude ! But this was a forgiveness which tended to penetrate the heart of the sinner with a sense of his own vileness, and of the
inflexible righteousness of Him, who, though he was
so merciful that he forgave their iniquity, yet did
not let their sin go unpunished, the bitter cup being
drunk by other lips than theirs, their salvation obtained by an atoning sacrifice that, though now
only faintly shadowed forth here, would turn the
heavens black with astonishment, and make earth
quake to her centre with horror !—a forgiveness
consistent with His sentence which had doomed the
sinner to die for his iniquity, and with the essential
holiness of His nature, "who is of purer eyes than
to behold evil," but yet who desireth not the death
of the sinner, but that he should turn from his
wickedness and live. These important truths were
all contained in the type of a crucified Saviour,
though probably but little understood by the majo-

rity of the people. One thing was, however, made intelligible to every humble and true believer, though, like the blind man in the Gospel, they could give little account of the meaning of the cure, that whereas they were unclean and excluded from the worship and service of God, now they were clean, they had free access restored to these forfeited privileges; and whereas they were subjected to those penal enactments which were the punishment of a transgression of the Jewish law, they were now no longer obnoxious to them, but restored to the favour of God; and the barrier which precluded all intercourse with their Maker being removed, they might " worship towards his holy temple, and give thanks at the remembrance of his holiness," which, having no longer any character of condemnation in it, was an object of adoring reverence now, and not of alarm and dread; and that now, lightened of the burden of the heavy load of guilt, they might begin to live a life of righteousness and holiness again. We can easily mark this happy change in the feelings of the believer under the Old Testament dispensation, who had tasted the blessedness of the man whose iniquities were forgiven and his sin covered, and to whom the Lord did not now impute sin; in place of seeking to hide himself as before *from* the presence of the Almighty, which is the natural sensation of a sinner, we hear him exclaim, " *Thou* art my hiding place, thou shalt preserve me from trouble, thou shalt compass me about with songs of deliverances," (Ps. xxxii.) What an alteration in the feelings does a sense of pardon occasion! And the earnest pleading of another who had " tasted that the Lord was gracious," but who had fallen again into dreadful sin, and transgressed the covenant, was not "Whither shall I flee from thy presence?" but " O ! cast me not away from thy presence, take not thy Holy Spirit from me." (Ps. li.) And again, in the 103rd Psalm, we have a glorious specimen of the outpourings of a pardoned and reconciled sinner's heart: "Bless the Lord, O ! my soul, and all that is within me bless his holy name ; bless the Lord, O my soul, and forget not all his benefits, who forgiveth all thine iniquities," &c.

True, all might not go through these interesting ceremonies with such a spiritual apprehension of their importance, and with such a lively feeling of their benefit.   Some would do it perhaps out of respect to their parents, from a reverence for old established habits and customs: some would go through them as a mere matter of form, to set their consciences at rest, by paying God the tribute of a small portion of their time, and small mark of their veneration, so as to enable them to live the rest of it at ease without him : some, perhaps, with an evil heart of unbelief, like Naaman, might so utterly discredit

the notion of such simple means ever attaining such
an important end, that they might turn from it with
contempt and disgust; and thus, from one or more
of these causes, many might deprive themselves of
the blessing and benefit of these divinely instituted
rites; still, every one will admit, their doing so was
a voluntary rejection or neglect of a privilege conferred upon them as a nation. The table had been
spread, the guests specially invited, and any one
who remained impenitent and unpardoned, disappointed thus the plans and intention of his God. None
would affirm they had not had the means of recovery
within their reach, and all those who did faithfully
employ them, found them effectual to the relief of
their necessities and the showing forth of God's
glory. There are many more remarkable sacrifices,
and singularly expressive types, which we can now
merely glance at, all several parts, as it were, of the
grand scheme of redemption; given to us separately, as an architect will show us different sections
of a building, and enter into the details, ere he ex-
hibits the complete model of the whole; and from
them we, even at this day of fuller knowledge, may
learn much; as the multiplication of sacrifices explain to us the extent and variety of the wants
of human nature, and may lead us, when we are
made sensible of the number and greatness of these
wants, to renew our application to our one great Foun-

tain, where all are supplied : and whilst it humbles
us in the dust, by disclosing our need of hourly expiation, it exalts the might and mercy of the Most
High, who has so graciously provided for all.　The
lamb, slain every morning and evening throughout
the year, informs us we have no right, in our natural
uncleanness, to approach our Maker, when we arise
in the morning to supplicate his blessing, and to beg
for his guidance and presence through the day, nor
yet to commend ourselves into his hands at night,
except through the merits and mediation of the Lamb
of God, who has said, " No man cometh unto the
Father except through me." By the double sacrifice of two every sabbath-day, we may also learn
how much more numerous, as well as how much
more holy, all our services were expected to be on
that day that God hath set apart for himself.　In
the mysterious and singular type of the ashes of the
red heifer, which tainted the clean, yet cleansed the
unclean from ceremonial defilements, we have set
before us Him " who was made sin for us, though he
knew no sin, but was holy, harmless, and undefiled,
that we might be made the righteousness of God in
Him." Also, in the sacrifices for the priesthood, we
have a strong intimation afforded us that no mere
mortal man was capable of being an offering acceptable to God, or available for man's salvation : " seeing he himself was compassed with infirmity, and by

reason hereof he ought for the people, so also for himself, to offer for sins ; and though Romanists indeed
think that every creature of human flesh they exalt
as a saint has a superabundance of merit to transfer
to others for their benefit, the Almighty did not deem
even the high priest of his choice and selection
worthy to be a propitiation for such purposes, but
considered him as one so deficient even on his own
account, as to need cleansing by burnt-offering : and
taught us thus to look for one more holy than *human*
nature could ever afford, and endued with powers, of
which it was utterly destitute for the purpose. Yet,
in the interesting and affecting similitude of the sacrifice of the scape-goat, and the two birds, (the one
set free, after being dipped in the blood of his fellow,) we are taught that though the atonement
which was to be made for our sin was to be *divine*,
as this alone was capable of achieving our salvation,
it was to be *human also*, a sameness in nature being
requisite, that one of the same flesh and blood of
those who had sinned, should make satisfaction for
the sin, and drink up the cup prepared for its crime.
But we can merely allude to these now, and commend the subject earnestly to the study of all, who
with chastened and humbled minds desire to obtain
a fund of instruction, and not merely engage in it for
the gratification of curiosity ; for we must now, according to our proposal, proceed to show, that though

F

many were thus the advantages and privileges of
the Jews under their dispensation, yet the multi-
plied variety and manifold particularity of their sacrifices, requiring a whole hecatomb of annual offerings, without one single day's intermission, argued
the weakness and unprofitableness thereof for effecting the entire and final purification of the human
nature from sin, and testified to their incompetency
for attaining it, for the law made nothing perfect :
for they served, says the apostle, " only unto the example and shadow of heavenly things, while as yet
the first tabernacle was standing," and whilst the
way into the holiest was not yet made manifest. " If,
then, the grand imposing event of our salvation
through Christ thus cast its shadow before it, like
that " from a great rock in a weary land," so full of
comfort and hope to the believer in those days,
what must not we enjoy, who possess the substance
of the things they hoped for, who have obtained the
things signified, of which these were but the sign ?
" For if that which was done away was glorious,
much more that which remaineth is glorious ;" for
all these converging rays of type and figure meet
in one centre, in the person of Jesus Christ, and him
crucified ; under the focus of whose concentrated
beams we live, on whom the ends of the world are
come. If the Jew, then, when he had offered gifts
and sacrifices for sin, according to the law, was enabled and entitled to feel such a degree of comfort

and peace, how much more shall the blood of Christ,
says the apostle, (Heb. vi. 9—14,) "Who through
the eternal Spirit offered himself without spot to
God, purge your conscience from dead works to
serve the living God, and afford us a source of far
superior peace and joy ! For the law having a shadow
of good things to come, and not the very image of
the things, can never with those sacrifices make the
corners thereunto perfect, for then would they not
have ceased to be offered, because that the wor-
shippers once purged should have had no more conscience of sin.   But in these sacrifices there is a remembrance again made of sin every year ; for it is
not possible that the blood of bulls and of goats
should take away sin : " It could not show forth
God's glory as a righteous Judge, if he was to allow
the guilty to escape, because they slew some innocent animal, whose value could bear no proportion
to the ransom of an immortal soul, and which could
give no consent to the substitution of itself in the
place of guilty ; which had nothing in common with
the nature of him whose person it was to represent,
and of whose crimes it was to bear the punishment ;
and though God, for a season, did consent to allow
of this substitution, yet it was always in a manner
to show that something more was intended ;' * but

* " What is Truth ?" By the Rev. Thomas White, St.
James's, Mary-le-bone.

Christ being come an high priest of good things to
come, when he had by himself purged our sins, for
ever sat down on the right hand of the majesty of
the Most High, for by one offering he hath perfected for ever them that are sanctified, having
forgiven us all our trespasses ; "for where remission
of these is, there remaineth no more offering for
sin." There is no longer any occasion for it. Papists,
indeed, crucify Christ afresh every time they offer
the mass, which our church most justly, in her thirty-
first article, stigmatises as " blasphemous fables and
dangerous deceits," and affirms most scripturally, that
Christ made upon the cross, " by his one oblation of
himself, once offered, a full, perfect, and sufficient
sacrifice, oblation, and satisfaction for the sins of the
whole world ;" for when he exclaimed there, " It is
finished," and with a loud voice yielded up the
ghost, the veil of the temple was rent in twain, from
the top to the bottom, the Holy Ghost thus signifying
to us that the way into the holiest *was* now obtained ;
for " Christ being made an high priest of good things
to come, not by the blood of bulls and goats, but by
his own blood, he entered into the holy place, having
obtained eternal redemption for us ; nor yet that he
should offer himself often, as the high priest entereth
into the holy place every year with blood of others,
for then must he often have suffered since the foundation of the world : but now once in the end of the

world he hath appeared, to put away sin by the
sacrifice of himself.

Our Lord has declared the incompetency of the
typical sacrifices to accomplish the intentions and
desires of the Almighty. " Sacrifice and offering
thou wouldest not, but a body hast thou prepared
me, in burnt-offerings and sacrifices for sin thou
hadst no pleasure. Then said I, Lo, I come (in
the volume of the book it is written of me) to do
thy will, O God: he taketh away the first that
he may establish the second, by the which will we
are sanctified by the offering of the body of Jesus
Christ once for all ; for by one offering he hath perfected for ever them that are sanctified," " through
the faith that is in him." Having, therefore, con-
tinues the apostle, " brethren, boldness to enter into
the holiest by the blood of Jesus, by a new and living
way which he hath consecrated for us through the
veil, that is to say, his flesh; and having an high
priest over the house of God, let us draw near, with
a true heart, in full assurance of faith, having our
hearts sprinkled from an evil conscience, and our
bodies washed with pure water :" " for we who were
afar off are made nigh by the blood of Jesus." (Eph.
i. 2.) The sword of the cherubim, which the fall
drew forth from its scabbard, and which turned every
way to ward off man's access to the tree of life in

an unholy state, has been sheathed in the heart of
our Redeemer : when he who was not willing that
any should perish, but that all should have eternal
life, cried out, " Awake, O sword, against my shepherd, and against the man that is my fellow, saith
the Lord of Hosts." When he gave his only begotten Son, that whosoever believeth in him might not
perish, but might have everlasting life, " I am the
good shepherd that giveth his life for the sheep,"
saith he, " which was made flesh, and dwelt among
us," for us men and for our salvation, and tasted
death for every man, " that as in Adam all die, even
so in Christ shall all be made alive." " Messiah
was cut off, but not for himself ;" (Dan. ix. 26 ;) " for
the transgression of my people was he stricken,"
(Isa. liii.) " When thou shalt make his soul an offering for sin, he shall see his seed, he shall prolong his
days, and the pleasure of the Lord shall prosper in
his hands : for he shall see of the travail of his soul,
and shall be satisfied." Here then the Christian is
shown in the Gospel the testamentary document
sealed with the blood of his Redeemer, (Heb. x.
15—17,) who is the Mediator of the New Testament, that by means of death for the redemption of
the transgressions that were under the Old, they
which are called might receive the promise of eternal inheritance; and the pledge of it, in a present

pardon and forgiveness, which restored him to access to his God, the author and giver of life, that we might become " followers of them, who through faith and patience inherit the promises," " if we held forth the beginning of our confidence stedfast unto the end." (Heb. vi. 12 ; iii. 14.) In the atonement of his Lord he is shown a pardon purchased for man by Christ, before any single human being had done one act that could deserve it at the hand of God, but not before every human being had so placed themselves by their sins, as rendered their salvation without it impossible : a pardon, too, to which man's merits can add nothing, and for which they in no way can prepare him : and from which his sins and demerits can detract naught : but one given purposely " to hide pride from men, and that no flesh should glory in *his* presence who is the end of the law for righteousness to every one that believeth, that of him, and from him, and to him, may be glory for ever and ever." Far, therefore, from keeping the atonement in the back ground, we, viewing it as the Alpha and the Omega, the beginning and the ending of our faith, place it prominently forward, as the grand object of primary and paramount importance to every human being; since it is none other than the very entrance into God's house below, and the golden key to the very gate of heaven above—the thing which first admits him as a member of Christ's church militant here on earth, and that which opens unto him the everlasting gates of the church glorified in heaven!

CHAPTER IV.

We have then ascertained it to be a fact, that the Jew, when he had gone through the significant ceremony of laying his hands upon the head of the appointed sacrifice, confessing over it his sins, was taught to believe his sins had passed over from his own person to that of the victim, who received the burden and bore the punishment of them in his stead ; for he was informed, upon doing so, " it was accepted *for him*, to make an atonement for him," and " his sin" was, in consequence, forgiven him." And we have also proved it to be a fact, amounting to demonstration, that our portion in the gospel is even a larger and a fuller one, besides being one much more comprehensive in its extension, and that " through this man," the Lord from heaven, " is preached unto *us* forgiveness of sins ; (Acts

xiii. 38, 39 ;) and by him all that believe are justified from all things from which they could not be justified by the law of Moses ;" therefore is our duty plain,
to be assured that if we by faith lay our hands upon
the head of Him "who bare our sins in his own
body on the tree, who was wounded for our transgressions, and bruised for our iniquities ;" that there
is that virtue in his blood for the expiation of sin,
that "though our sins be as scarlet, they shall be
white as snow, though they be red as crimson, they
shall be as wool ;" "for the blood of Jesus Christ
his Son cleanseth us from all sin." (Isa. i. ; 1 John
i.) Though our sacrifice is not set forth before our
eyes as it was formerly to the Jews, it is not the less
sure and stedfast ; and we "who walk by faith and
not by sight," are not to expect any *visible* demonstration to the senses that the grand end is accomplished, but to believe *it is*, on the credit of God's
word alone ; for " the righteousness which is of
faith speaketh "on this wise, Say not in thine
heart, who shall ascend into heaven? (that is, to bring
Christ down from above) or who shall descend into
the deep ? (that is, to bring Christ up again from
the dead ;) but what saith it? the word is very nigh
thee, even in thy mouth and in thy heart, that is,
the word of faith which we preach, that if thou
shalt confess with thy mouth the Lord Jesus, and
shalt believe in thine heart that God hath raised

him from the dead, thou shalt be saved ; for with
the heart man believeth unto righteousness, and
with the mouth confession is made unto salvation."
Therefore has our church very appropriately demanded of her children that they shall every
sabbath day make an open and *audible* confession
of their belief in Jesus in their creed, and in " the
forgiveness of sins ;" a truth made evident to us in
Scripture by every form of expression and every variety of similitude that can make it intelligible, from
the simplest, that the wayfaring man, though a fool,
shall not err in comprehending, to the strongest,
that can give satisfaction, to the profoundest intellect that examines the subject with attention.   We
are there told, that not only the things we have done
which we ought not to have done are forgiven,
(Col. ii. 13,) " Having forgiven you all your trespasses." " I write unto you, little children, because
your sins are forgiven you for his name's sake ;"
but those we have left undone that we ought to
have done are remitted.   (Acts ii. 38.) " Repent,
and be baptized every one of you, in the name of
Christ Jesus for the remission of sins ;" (x. 43,)
" To him give all the prophets witness, that through
his name whosoever believeth in him shall receive remission of sins." And not only are we
told they are forgiven and remitted, but that they
are blotted out, so that they shall never appear as

charges against us again ; (Col. ii. 14,) " Blotting
out the handwriting of offences that was against
us, which is contrary to us, and took it out of the
way, nailing it to his cross." And not only are we
informed that by it we are outwardly washed and
cleansed, " according to his mercy he saved us by
the washing of regeneration and renewing of the
Holy Ghost." (Titus iii 5.) And he that is
" washed needeth not save to wash his feet," (John
xiii.) but is clean every whit, and ye are clean,"
&c., but that we are inwardly purified by an inter-
nal purification. " When he (Jesus) had by himself
purged our sins, he for ever sat down on the right
hand of God." St. Peter, writing to unfruitful believers, says, they have " forgotten that they were
purged from their old sins." And not these expressions are even deemed sufficient to express our
privileges and emancipation from the guilt and thral-
dom of sin under the Gospel, but we are told we are
bought and *redeemed* with a price ; " Not with corruptible things as silver and gold, but with the
precious blood of Christ, as of a lamb without blemish and without spot." (1 Cor. vi. 20, 1 Pet. i. 18
and 19.) And as sin is the moral sickness of the
soul, we are told the heavenly Physician has undertaken our cure—' by whose stripes we are *healed*,"
—so that either we are driven to the alternative, to
allow that all language is inadequate to make *any*

truth plain to us, words are so destitute of all definite sense, as to be unable to convey *any* distinct meaning to us, or that the believer in Jesus Christ is to understand " that he is washed, he is sanctified, he is justified, in the name of Christ Jesus, and by the Spirit of God." But besides the confession of our faith that is insisted on, the Scripture mentions another duty equally necessary under the law and under the Gospel, confession of our sins : " If we confess our sins, he is faithful and just to forgive us our sins," &c. (1 John i. 9 ;) and the reason of this is too obvious to need much explanation, since, as none but *sinners* stand in need of an atonement, or require forgiveness, for any to claim a share in it, who were not of *this* class, were as unnecessary as it would be abused. And were there one being of human flesh who could lay his hand upon his heart and say, I have *never* sinned in word, thought, or deed against God, for such an one to lay his hand upon the head of a sacrifice for sins were an idle mockery ! But as God knows there is *no man* who can say so, for " there is not a just man upon earth that doeth good and sinneth not," he says, " if we say that we have no sin, we deceive ourselves, and the truth is not in us," and we make him a liar who hath said, " there is none righteous, . no not one:" He demands of every one who approaches to avail himself of the blood of sprinkling,

that he shall make an honest, unfeigned, unequivo-
cating confession of his sins, and acknowledgment
of his need of a Saviour and of pardon. Thus
Joshua, under the law, exhorted the guilty Achan,
" My son, give glory to the God of Israel, and
make confession unto him." Thus the psalmist expresses his sense of the duty and benefit of it:
" When I kept silence, my bones waxed old through
my roaring all the day long. I acknowledged my
sin unto thee, and mine iniquity have I not hid; I
said, I will confess my transgressions unto the Lord,
and so thou forgavest the iniquity of my sin." (Ps.
xxxii.) Thus the prophet Jeremiah (iii. 13.)
admonishes backsliders, " Only acknowledge thine
iniquity that thou hast transgressed against the
Lord thy God." And Hosea, v. 15, describes the
Lord as waiting and looking out for this in his people, " I will go and return to my place till they
acknowledge their offence." And this is the only
way we ever can glorify God now; not by our sin-
less purity, but by repentance, when his mercy is
extolled as the *only* cause of our salvation, when
we own that "not by works of righteousness that
we have done, but according to his mercy he saved
us," (Titus,) by letting mercy rejoice over judgment, and grace abound over sin. Here Rome has
in this, as in many things, defrauded God of
his rights, and, stepping in between man and his

Maker, insists on this homage being rendered to her ministers first; and into the hands of fallen sinful man has she committed this dangerous and demoralizing duty; but our scriptural church, which is built only on " the foundation of the apostles and prophets," and which never " teaches for doctrines the commandments of men," has rejected this false assumption of a right which belongs to God only, and whilst she demands of every member of her communion that they shall make a public and general confession that they are sinners, and consequently need that salvation she holds out for all who repent and believe in Jesus, she leaves the description of particulars and confidential disclosures by each man of the plague of his own heart for *his* ear alone who can deliver us from its guilt, without being contaminated by the details. Nor is confession the easy duty some imagine; for though nothing can be more easy than the mere *verbal* expression of sinfulness, there is nothing more difficult to human nature, and nothing to which we have a greater aversion, than coming to a free admission, and being brought to a deep-felt sense of our sin, and self-abhorrence of it. " The heart is deceitful above all things, and desperately wicked, who can tell it?" and to be able to unveil *its* abominations, and to look at it in all its real and hideous deformity, and instead of trying to excuse and

lessen the enormity of our guilt, to be fully conscious of it, to take God's part against ourselves
in it, and to own and feel not only that we have
sinned, but that we are utterly *inexcusable* in having done so, and can shift the blame on no other
shoulders than our own, far less lay it upon our
situation, constitution, or any such thing, which is,
in fact, transferring it to our Maker, is a state of mind
few ever attain to ; and of those who do, how seldom
is it that even these exhibit it in all its genuine earnestness and depth of sincerity, as one would expect !

Our proud hearts revolt from the necessity of
always thus approaching God on the ground of
penitence only ; and cannot be persuaded that
whatever advances they may make in all other respects, they never, " till this corruptible shall put
on incorruption," can advance one step which shall
relieve them from the necessity of approaching God
always as sinners, who have no right to approach
him in any other way, save for the sake of the merits
of Jesus Christ our Lord.   And from the first hour
we enter into life, till faith is lost in sight, it forms
one of the most difficult parts of the Christian's conflict, though one of the most improving too, as this
constant and daily putting off self, by this humiliat-
ing duty, and putting on Christ, forms a sluice to
let off pride, where, if a man thinketh himself to be
something when he is nothing, he is thus habitually

taught to see that "he is poor and wretched and naked and miserable," by its constantly thus bringing his sins to light, and making him slay them thus before the Lord. And as it is a duty so irksome and painful to the soul, there is none which men more frequently neglect and shrink from; and often the unyielding resistance of our nature will give in to nothing but stress of trial, and our being cast into the fiery furnace of affliction, when the heart that would neither bow nor break will, like iron, bend beneath the influence of a sin-disclosing, heart-searching process of suffering, and we are " made to possess the iniquities of our youth," (Job xiii. 26,) by the Holy Spirit bringing all things to our remembrance, and convincing us thus of our sin, and humbling us into submission. Hence the *necessity* of *tribulation*, and the *reason* of the close connexion of *it* with *believing*, we may observe throughout the Bible. If we only examine the Epistles, we must see how it is interwoven with the whole structure of some of the apostle's discourses, and how they in others wind up their definitions and descriptions of *faith* by attaching *tribulation* to it, as part of the Christian's portion they embrace on believing. See Rom. v. 3; Heb. xii.; James i. 4, 12; 1 Peter i. 6, 7; which explains to us the meaning and importance of our Lord's words, "Every sacrifice must be salted with *fire* as well as salt;" and truly, that which has

been salted with grace (viz. salt) is well prepared
for, and will never shrink from, this further conformity to the Image of their divine Head, the fiery
trial of suffering, who was " a man of sorrows, and
acquainted with grief."

But difficult and painful as a true confession
of sin is, we must not therefore look upon it in
the light of a mere degrading and burdensome
duty; for, if viewed aright, it is one of the
most important and soul-reviving ones we can
be engaged in, and there is none in which we can
have holier and purer communion with God. *Praise*
is, indeed, a higher and happier exercise, but *confession* is the preparation, the foundation, the inseparable attendant upon it; and perhaps it is not too
fanciful to suppose that the *cloven* tongues of fire
which sat upon the heads of the disciples, were
meant to signify the song of the Christian must ever
consist of two notes, to make up one harmonious
chord in the ears of the Lord God of Sabaoth, humiliation and thanksgiving. And to give it all the
dignity and importance it deserves, let us remember
that penitence is now the only link which can reunite
man to his Maker; the tie of *innocence* being irrepa-
rably brok en.

We come into the world even as those who need
the washing of baptism to fit them for approach
ing God. And none can, from their own sinlessness and goodness, expect a love of compla-

cency to beam forth upon them from God in
their natural state: all they can look for, is a
love of holy compassion; and the heart that stands
out in resolute rebellion, and refuses to own itself a
fit subject for the exercise of his divine mercy
towards it, must be, in fact, pushing back the hand
stretched out to raise it out of the mire and clay
into which its transgressions have plunged it. And
in our restored and recovered state, the love of the
Father comes forth to us, not because of our *own
deserts*, for, says the Apostle, " I know that in *me*,
that is in *my flesh*, dwelleth *no good thing*," but
because of the work that the Holy Spirit *has wrought
in us*." He that abideth in me, and I in him,
the same bringeth forth much fruit, for *without me*
ye can do *nothing*," and "herein is my Father glorified, that ye bear much fruit." And " ye are
my friends, if ye do whatsoever I command you."
And my Father himself loveth you, *because ye have*
loved *me*, and have believed that I came forth from
God. (John, ch. xv. and xvi.) And, " he that
loveth *me* shall be loved of *my Father*."

We have just said there is but *one* way left, in which
we can " give God glory," and that is, by *now will-
ingly confessing* our sins—but no, there is one other
way : but God grant none who read this, may ever prefer *it !* If we rebelliously and obstinately refuse to
give God glory by this *voluntary* tribute now, as

the only reparation we can make for our offence, we shall be *compelled* to give it, whether we will or no, when we receive the sentence upon our souls as those "*who repented not to give* God glory, Rev. xvi. 9, pronounced then by men and angels for our *condemnation*, in place of our own lips now pronouncing this acknowledgment, that we are sinners, for our *salvation*.

But we trust all will avert from themselves this awful fate by a prompt and free confession and repentance. Now "to-day, whilst it is called to-day, if ye will hear his voice, harden not your hearts, for "if we confess our sins, he is faithful and just to forgive us our sins, and to cleanse us from all unrighteousness." He is "*faithful*" to his sure word of *promise*. " Whosoever believeth in him (Christ) *shall receive* remission of sins," for what he hath promised he is able also to perform ; he is "*just*" in doing so, as " he *can* now be just, and the justifier of them that believe in Jesus," seeing it is become a righteous and just thing in him, and in strict conformity with the word of truth ; *as* an atonement has been made for the offence, the debt man owed has been paid, and man is now restored to his right place with God, in which his favour can beam forth again upon him, to return to him with loving-kindness and with tender mercy, as saith the prophet Micah, ch. vii. 18, 19, " Who is a God like unto thee, that

pardoneth iniquity, and passeth by the transgression
of the remnant of the people ? He retaineth not his
anger for ever, because he delighteth in mercy. He
will turn again, he will have compassion upon us, and
thou wilt cast all their sins into the depths of the sea.''

But it may naturally be asked here, if the Jews
then, under the Old Testament dispensation, did
obtain thus a knowledge of the forgiveness of sins,
when they had offered those gifts and sacrifices
upon the altar according to the law, " which can
never take away sin," who looked through them
in prospective faith at "the Lamb of God which
taketh away the sin of the world ;" and if we, who
look back retrospectively at the redemption our
Lord accomplished on the cross, " by whom we
have now received the atonement," Rom. v. 11,
do obtain, in a much fuller and higher sense, " remission of our sins, and all the benefits of Christ's
most precious blood-shedding ;" why, if these
things are so, is it that it is a truth so little known
by most, so little understood by any, and even de-
nied by some who profess and call themselves
Christians ? The reason may be, that so general
a mistake exists, as to the nature of the pardon
conveyed to us in the atonement, such an Antino-
mian sense having been so often attached to it,
which led to gross and grievous abuses of it, that
the idea it engenders licentiousness has become so

prevalent as to lead to a natural and almost commendable jealousy on the subject in the minds of
many true friends to holiness, which makes them
averse to examining it themselves, and studiously
anxious to exclude it from the notice of others,
for fear of those mischievous effects following, which
have too often tracked its progress : and many have
been led thus to cast away the precious with the
vile, and hence to reject the subject entirely, ima-
gining that embracing any part of it involved them
in receiving all the errors of the system ; and think-
ing it was better to remain themselves, and keep
their hearers all their life in suspense on the subject, than to run the risk of receiving or propounding
a doctrine so beset with dangers : and consequently
they have so tied it up with conditions, or explained
it away with modifications, that it is a greater
wonder, perhaps, that any ever attain to a comfortable apprehension of it, than that so few do.

Were the pardon, which we are told is contained
in the atonement, such an one as, after it has been
once obtained, sets the sinner above the necessity
of ever applying for it again, as this would plainly
militate against our Lord's command, when ye
pray, say, daily, forgive us our trespasses, and it
would be at once discarded by every believer in
sound writ as one quite contrary to the authority
of its divine Author, who, knowing that as there

was not a day, nay, nor an hour in the day, in which
man's absolute freedom from sin would render the
use of it unnecessary, so there was not one that
would exonerate him from the duty of asking for it;
were it one, either, like that which the Romanist
purchases beforehand, to obtain by anticipation a
pardon for the sins he intends to commit, or which
he may involuntarily fall into, the manifest absur-
dity of it would cause it to be rejected at once by
every intelligent human being, who would feel it
as much an insult upon the sense the Almighty had
given him, as upon the majesty of him who cannot
be mocked ; or were it one that, by pretending to insure a man's eventual safety, independent of his own
exertions, and irrespective of his own conduct,—a
pardon which could be worn secretly as an amulet
to preserve his [as a charmed life, into whatever
scene he should presumptuously rush, or any sins
into which he might unfortunately fall; such a one
insuring ultimate safety, and granting an intermediate license for sin, every mind in the least degree
enlightened by the Holy Spirit, or acquainted with
the holy character of him with whom we have to
do, or that listened to the natural voice of conscience even within him, would spurn, as none of
that "wisdom which cometh down from above
which is first *pure*, &c.; but as the impious sug-
gestion of the father of lies, and of all abominations,

assured it was a pardon as impossible for a righteous God to grant, as for any upright mind to receive; but the pardon pointed out to us in the atonement, though one so perfect as to contain in itself the power of instantaneous and complete ablution for the soul, the moment it is applied by faith to the penitent conscience, no more sets us above the necessity of again seeking for a repetition of it, the moment we fall into sin, or again contract any defilement, than the lamb slain in the morning by the Israelites to cleanse their conscience from dead works, that they might walk before God in holiness and righteousness all the day, exonerated them from the obligation of offering another in the evening afresh, to wash them thoroughly from their wickedness that they had committed through the day; but leaves imposed upon us the duty, or rather permits us the privilege, of returning, upon every new motion of sin in the heart, to lay our heads by faith upon the head of Him who made his soul an offering for sin, confessing our transgressions, and owning our need of his purifying blood, and beseeching the Father, for the great love wherewith he hath loved us, in giving his dear Son to die for us, to receive us graciously, and love us freely, and to let his anger be turned away from us in his name, and for *his* sake. No, its efficacy does not extend beyond the present moment, and to-day's forgiveness may not

be laid up for to-morrow's wants; but, like the
manna, it must be gathered fresh every day;
nay, every moment we must " come boldly to the
throne of grace, that we may obtain mercy, and
find grace to help us *in every time of need*," from
Him who is exalted to *give* repentance and remission
of sins to His people ; and is as much required by
the most advanced saint to wipe away the least
spot of sin that disfigures that fine linen, white
and clean, which is the righteousness of saints,
the garment which he shall wear when he enters
heaven, as it is by the vilest sinner the first moment
he draws near God's mercy-seat in all his sinfulness
and impurity. So far is it either from being a pardon
which will be given us by God, to justify us upon His
discovering in us certain good feelings and spiritual
graces infused into us, which may induce Him to
show us mercy, or entitle us to expect it at his
hands, as Romanists, and alas ! as Romanized Protestants, assert. We are told that Christ came not to
call the righteous, but sinners to repentance, for " he
hath filled the *hungry* with good things, but the
rich he hath sent empty away ;" for Christ is become
of no effect unto whosoever is justified by the law,
for they are fallen from grace ; and so far is it from its
being the case, that it is because God perceives
some good thing in us to attract his regard, or procure his favour, we are told, " God hath concluded
all under sin, that the promise by faith of Jesus

Christ might be given to all them that believe."
Therefore, " knowing that a man is not justified by
the works of the law, but by the faith of Christ
Jesus, even we have believed in Christ Jesus,
that we might be justified by the faith of Christ,
and not by the works of the law," says the apostle
in Gal. 2d, 3d, 4th, and 5th chapters; and as it is a
justification which rests on the merits of Christ
Jesus alone, and not on our poor pretensions, it
forbids any to doubt, who, like the thief on the
cross, have no time left them for giving a testimony
to the sincerity of their faith, by adding to it virtue,
and to virtue knowledge, and to knowledge tempe-
rance, &c., as it also forbids any to indulge in vain
glory who are permitted to go on from grace to
grace, and from strength to strength, till they appear
in Zion. For where is boasting then? it is excluded, for we are saved by grace, and *that* not of ourselves, but it is the gift of God, not of works, lest
any man should boast.

It is one of the worst charges against the
Church of Rome, that she maintains that the
atonement is incomplete for our salvation, till
we have added our little quota of merits to
make up for its deficiencies. But that this is
a charge by no means confined to Rome alone, we
have but to look into a number of Protestant books
of the present day, and listen to many Protestant
preachers, to discover. As we find the Gospel by

them so neutralized and weakened by the reser-
vations and exceptions attached to it—the silver
so become dross, the wine so mixed with water,
that when people, allured by universality of the
invitations, the earnestness of the call to come
unto Jesus, draw near, the food is, at it were,
snatched up from before their eyes, or they are met
with such demands for pre-requisite qualifications in
themselves, that what is given on the one hand seems
taken away from them with the other ; and, after all
their highly-raised hopes and expectations, they
find they are in reality little better off than before.
For instance, by some they are told they must prove
their personal interest in Christ, ere they are entitled to a share in the virtue of His atonement.
That this is a perfectly consistent statement on the
part of those churches which limit the extent of
Christ's sacrifice to the elect alone, none can dispute, as in this case we *do* need some private in-
terpretation of the Scriptures to our own case,
some secret intimation to ourselves as individuals,
besides " the record that God gave of his Son, and
this in the record *that God hath given to us*
eternal life, and this life is in his Son," ere we can
know that we are of that select number for whom
the table is spread, and not of " the poor, for whom
nothing is provided." But it is surely an utterly
inadmissible proposition on the part of ministers

of the Church of England, who has taught each child of *her* communion to lisp from its cradle, in its catechism, its belief "in Jesus Christ, who hath redeemed me *and all mankind,*" and requires every one of the members of *her* congregation to give thanks every sabbath "for the redemption of the WORLD by our Lord Jesus Christ;" leaving none of them in uncertainty as to whether "they have any part or lot in the matter, but assuring each human being that his being bone of man's bone, and flesh of his flesh, and who approaches as one "who has erred and strayed from God's ways like lost sheep," and has offended against His holy laws;" that they are included in the number of those for whom Christ died, that *they have an interest* in the benefit of his atonement, of which no human sophistry can deprive them !

Some, again, deprive all the declarations and promises of mercy of their weight by telling us they are intended only for *believers;* and therefore, till we have ascertained to a certainty that our faith is true and sound, and we are indeed and in truth of *their* number, we are in no way entitled to the benefit of them. But so far is this from being the case, that we are told, in place of man's believing penitence having wrung the mercy from his Maker's hand after his fall, and, in consequence of this, a Redeemer was appointed, that our redemption was contrived by the determinate counsel and foreknowledge of God; nay, mystically accomplished by " the Lamb of God slain before the foundation of the world," before man was called into being by the goodness and loving-kindness of God alone, who, seeing the end from the beginning, foresaw man would fall, and thus provided a means for his recovery in the mysterious arrangements of the Divine providence; and that when, after a long trial of man on earth, it was proved " the world by wisdom knew not God," *nor* repented them of the evil of their ways, for that when He looked down from heaven to see if there was any that would understand and seek after God, He saw that there was no man, and wondered that there was no intercessor; therefore His own arm wrought salvation for them, in place of man peni-tently on his knees supplicating it at his Maker's hands, or showing such gifts and graces as inclined him to relent and turn away His wrath from them. And has He changed the mode of his procedure now? No, by no means! "As it was in the begin-ning, *is now*, and ever shall be, world without end," God hath concluded all *in unbelief*, that he might have mercy upon all; and so far from this mercy being given only to believers, Christ came to seek and save the lost. "He died for the *ungodly*, the *just* for the *unjust*," " for they that be *whole* need not a physician, but they that are sick." Believers

are, no doubt, in a special manner partakers of the
promises, and enjoyers of the gift of life in Christ
Jesus ; but to say all this is restricted to them, and
intended to be confined to them only, is a very
misleading statement, or a strange persuasion of
the truth.   Whilst they are indeed walking in the
light, "they are to be holding forth the word of
life," "letting their light so shine in the eyes of
men, that they, seeing their good works, might glorify
their Father which is in heaven," as proving what is
that good and perfect and acceptable will of God,
"who will have *all* men to be saved and come to
the knowledge of the truth. (1 Tim. ii. 4.)   They are
to consider themselves as samples and patterns
shown to others of what God would wish all men
to be.   "Neither pray I for them alone," says
our Lord, "but for them also which shall believe
on me through their word, that they all may be one,
as thou, Father, art in me, and I in thee, that they
also may be one in us, and *that the world may believe*
that thou hast sent us."   Nor does our Lord, saying,
in a preceding text, he prays *not* for the world, in-
validate the force of this ; for we may easily conceive
he means by this, that those who should, after all
this, remain obstinately hardened and impenitent,
were no longer objects of that mercy they had de-
spised and trampled on, and that they who rejected
Him, He would plead for no more, and his Father

would reject at the last day. And so far are we from being entitled to say that only for those that *received* it the gift was intended, or ever meant to be given to them, that St. John says, (1 John ii. 2,) " He is the propitiation for our sins," speaking as a believer, " and not for ours only, but also for the sins of the whole world ;" as says St. Paul to Timothy, (1 Tim. iv. 10,) " We trust in the living God, who is the living Saviour of all men, specially of those that believe."

It is indeed true that St. Paul, in his epistles, *is* addressing believers, for they were written to converts and professing Christians ; but he is by no means intending that what he said was exclusively theirs, and to be hedged in and confined to their use only! He was more fully explaining to them among whom he had gone preaching the kingdom of God, those things which were most surely believed among them, that they might know the certainty of those things wherein they had been before instructed, and be themselves better able thus to understand their value, as well as to explain it to others, that *they* might likewise believe to the saving of their souls. He was giving them, as it were, a catalogue and fuller description of the precious jewels he was entrusting to their care as their invaluable legacy, to be by them carefully preserved, and faithfully transmitted to the church, as her heir-loom for all generations ;

and what he says of the nature and value of these
blessings belongs as much to us, who have believed
on them through their word, and to all men now
living, as it did to them.

Another objection often urged by those who do
not see, or dislike the idea of pardon being contained
in the atonement, is, that were men assured God
had, in the sacrifice for sin, made satisfaction for
human iniquity, there would be no motive to men
for repentance: in fact, man's ingenuity seems to
have been racked to know how best to unnerve the
hand that would stretch itself forth to *lay* hold of
the hope set before us in the Gospel, or to deprive
its promises of all force in laying hold of the soul.
Alas for poor fallen human nature! low as it *is*
fallen, they would degrade it still farther, by showing that no other motive than selfishness ever can find
a place in the heart. Whereas we believe there
can be no cure for its natural selfishness, nothing
which can cast it out from its possession of our
souls within, but this doctrine, which takes away
every motive for its continuance, deprives us of all
inducement to resort to it, and admits of a repentance which needs not to be repented of—a genuine,
unfeigned, heartfelt sorrow, which can never be felt
as long as we are uncertain of the feelings and intentions of our God towards us; for, till then, sorrow must be so mixed up with fear and dread

of the consequences of our sin, that our motives in
repentance may have so much of self-interest in
them, and desire by its means to obtain salvation,
as to render its sincerity very questionable. Till
we know sin is forgiven, we are unable either to
estimate the amount of our transgressions, or to
acknowledge their extent, as no one dares to look
his sin in the face, or to admit the degree of it, till
then : and therefore they resort for relief to every
subterfuge, and take refuge in every invention they
can desire, to cheat themselves into the belief their
sin is not so great as they thought, and that God is
not so greatly to be feared as some imagine : and
hence arises the temptation to make light of sin, or to
lessen the idea of the divine displeasure against it :
or to cloak and hide it to exculpate themselves : to
blind them to the truth, and thus obtain a temporary relief themselves, or impart it to others. Like
the bankrupt who feels an aversion and dread of
looking closely into his affairs when he knows he
has no funds sufficient to meet the demands of his
creditors, and who prefers living in a fool's paradise
of false peace, rather than have his eyes opened to
see irretrievable ruin ; but if a friend possessed of
ample means for the purpose placed, these at his
disposal, and assured him of release from all his
difficulties, he would no longer hesitate to examine
into the amount of his debts himself, or to submit

his books to his inspection; just as a knowledge
of the forgiving mercy of God sweeps away all those
refuges of lies men have fled to, and leaves them no
longer any inducement to hide the truth from their
own eyes, or attempt to conceal it from God. And,
on the contrary, *now* they can bare their bosom to
His inspection, and cry, " Search me O Lord, and
try my thoughts, prove me, and examine my heart,
look well if there be any way of wickedness in me."
For as they can look a Saviour in the face, and see
the handwriting that was against them nailed to
his cross, and for ever wiped out as an accusation
against them, they can now take God's part fear-
lessly against it. They can now stand on His side
against themselves, and feel all their sympathies are
with him who hateth the sin indeed, but has no
pleasure in the death of the sinner, but rather that
he should turn from his wickedness and live. When
God has given us " the new heart and the new
spirit," promised us under the Gospel-covenant, and
" has taken away the stony heart out of our flesh,
and given us the heart of flesh," *then* do we remember our own evil ways, and our doings that
were not good, and *then* do we, as it is expressively
described, " loathe ourselves in our own sight,
for our iniquities and our abominations;" (Ezek.
xxxvi. 26—31 ;) for when we find it is *our* sins
that caused the sufferings of the Lord of glory, and

are assured of our *personal* concern in it, then and then only we are " pricked to the heart;" we " look upon Him whom *we have* pierced, and¦mourn for Him, as one that mourneth for his only son, and are in bitterness as one that is in bitterness for his first-born." (Zech. xii. 10.) If the atonement does not include pardon in its gift, we may well be at a loss to know what it does contain. And if redemption merely procured us *a chance* of our being ultimately forgiven by God, as some express it, then are we little better off than the Hindoo devotee who casts himself beneath the wheels of Juggernaut, the Mahometan pilgrim who toils to Mecca, or the Romanist who lacerates his body to obtain or merit it ; except that *we* gain our pardon by a less laborious process, and at a less expense of physical sufferings; but if we merely attain to a vague hope that, for these things, God will extend his mercy to us, viz. if we have fulfilled certain conditions, or can exhibit certain frames and feelings of mind, it is undeniable that we are very little further on the road to that peace of God which passeth all understanding, than they are.

If the atonement of Jesus Christ has not procured us the forgiveness of our sins, we may well inquire of those that deny it, what else *is to do it?* And when is this blessed and important end to be obtained ? We are not to look for anything more

to be done for us on earth to accomplish it; for we
are expressly told, "there remaineth *no more* sacrifice for sins" to those who neglect and despise *this,*
or distrust and set at naught its efficacy for the
purpose.   Still less are we to expect any more to be
done for us in heaven ; there, indeed, is the Lamb of
God seen before the throne, but not as if ready to be
offered up, "for this He did once for all ;" but "as
it has been slain," and remaining a perpetual memorial in the sight of God, and for the exercise of
faith in man, that He hath "put away sins by the
sacrifice of himself," and having "finished transgression, made an end of sin, and brought in everlasting righteousness"—"Christ being raised from
the dead dieth *no more*"—Surely none can be so
senseless as to expect any expiation to be made for
them at the day of judgment; for then, indeed,
Christ cometh with clouds, and every eye shall see
him, and they also which pierced Him, and all the
kingdoms of the earth shall wail because of him,"
for then the day of grace and mercy is ended, and
(Rev. vi. 16, 17,) "the great day of his wrath
is come,"—the wrath of *the Lamb.*   The day of
judgment, as its very *name* imports, is a day of
strictly giving to every one according to their
deserts—a trial to succeed a long dispensation of forbearing mercy.   We might learn a lesson from what
takes place in courts of justice on earth, on this

head, where men rest their hopes of acquittal upon the absence of proof of guilt, or evidence of innocence of the charge they can produce, and not upon the character and feelings of the judge, for they know he sits there an administrator of the laws, and must pass sentence according as it is proved men have been innocent or guilty of their breach, and not according to his own tender-heartedness, or the mercifulness of his disposition; and to this our Lord refers, when he says, "He that rejecteth me, and receiveth not my words," (His gracious invitations and entreaties to turn from the evil of our ways and come unto him,) "hath one that judgeth him : *the word* that I have spoken, *the same* shall judge him in the last day." (John xii. 48.) All His present mercy shall then rise up in judgment against him, and turn to a testimony against him, for the Father judgeth no man, but hath committed all judgment unto the Son, and hath given Him authority to execute judgment because he is the Son of Man : "Marvel not at this, for the hour is coming, in the "which all ^that are in the graves shall hear his voice and shall come forth ; they that have *done good* unto the resurrection of life, and they that have *done evil* unto the resurrection of damnation." Therefore that will not be the season for man to seek and supplicate, or to expect pardon.—" *Now* is the accepted time, *now* is the day of salvation." " Seek the Lord while

he *may be found*, call upon Him while *He is near :*
Let the wicked forsake his ways, and the unrighte-
ous man his thoughts, and let him return unto the
Lord, and *He will* have mercy upon him, and to our
God, for *He will abundantly pardon.*" (Isaiah lv. 6.)

CHAPTER V.

HAVING, then, arrived at the important point, that " God hath reconciled us to himself by the death of his Son," who hath loved us and washed us from our sins in his own blood, we have obtained a firm foundation whereon to plant our feet ; here then let us pause a few moments, thank God and take courage, reflect upon the steps by which we have come to this blessed conclusion, and contemplate the goodly prospect it unfolds before us.

Had it pleased God simply to announce this to us as a fact, to be by all men believed on the credit of his word alone, " that he was in Christ, reconciling the world unto himself, not imputing their trespasses unto them, having made Him to be made sin for them ;" to stand in their place as a sinner, and receive the punishment of their sins, that they

" might be made the righteousness of God in Him ;"
might stand in his place as righteous persons, being
justified from all their iniquity through his blood—
had he merely declared this to be a fact, upon the
strength of which he commanded all men to return to Him now, as to a reconciled Father who
had cast away the weapons of his wrath against
them, and having testified in His desire, that all
men should have eternal life, by giving his Son
a ransom for all, had proclaimed a period of
universal amnesty, during which temporary period,
or day of grace, all men were as freely permitted
to come to him as Adam was before his fall, not on
the ground, like him, of being acceptable from
their sinlessness, but on the ground of being accepted for the alone sake of the merits and mediation of Christ our Saviour ; the knowledge of this
fact, containing, as it did, all that was necessary for
their comfort here and their hope hereafter, whilst
it made heaven ring aloud with ' Glory to God in
the highest, on earth peace, good-will toward men,'
was enough to make earth shout aloud in reply,
" Hosanna to the Son of David."

> " Worthy the Lamb that died, *they* cry,
>   To be exalted thus :
> Worthy the Lamb, *our* lips reply,
>   For he was slain for *us* !"

Had the announcement ended here, and had the information extended no further, it would have been as fruitless as it would have been presumptuous, for creatures like us, "crushed before the moth,". to have inquired deeper into the subject. But since the Almighty, with a most merciful consideration for our feelings, and with a most gracious regard to our natural desire to hear more on a subject so nearly concerning our highest interests, has been pleased to give us an account of His ways, sufficiently plain for our finite minds to understand, of all that they ever *can* understand of " the great mystery of godliness, God manifest in the flesh," and has condescended to tell us what means were employed to accomplish our deliverance—nay, in some measure to explain to us why such means were found necessary ; we are bound to give earnest heed to the things that are spoken, assured that they cannot be attended to without benefit, or neglected without loss to our souls. For therein, we are told, " is the righteousness of God revealed from faith to faith ;" " even the righteousness which is by faith of Christ Jesus." By this revelation of his ways and doings, he is pleased to " justify the ways of God to man ;" and to vindicate the uprightness and justness of His plans and proceedings to his creatures ; lest any should be at a loss to reconcile his receiving back the sinner

again to his favour, with His declaration, that " He
will not justify the wicked," " the soul that sinneth
it shall die." For as He is too holy to look upon
iniquity, so *no man* could ever hope to see *His* face
and live," whom the pure in heart *alone* shall see,
and thus, according to all our notions of moral
rectitude, as sin and holiness were as incompatible
as light and darkness, life and death, the one must
always flee before the face of the other, God and
man seemed hopelessly and eternally separated.
Men must thus ever fly from the presence of God,
or God depart from man, " who had left off to be-
have himself wisely, and to do good." Man, we have
already fully shown, could do nothing on his part to
reverse the sentence, but every action of his life
was only fitted to confirm it more decidedly. Had
God on his part in these circumstances retracted
his word, and recalled his denunciations upon sin,
so as to allow of the sinner's approach to him in
all his uncleanness, such an act of unfaithfulness to
His word, on the part of the Governor of the uni-
verse, would have been man's moral ruin, for all
the goodness and all the glory of his other perfections, I speak it with reverence, could never have
struck man blind to this defect in the one grand
point of all, or done away the injury of letting
him imagine that God, by showing mercy at the
expense of his truth, had compromised His word,

which would have subverted all confidence in his
Maker's word for ever: and by letting him see
sin treated with impunity, in spite of all God's
denunciations against it, would have abated all his
feelings as to the deadly nature of sin, and as to
the essential holiness' of God's character. As we
may observe in human affairs, a weak and tem-
porizing policy in domestic and national concerns,
unexecuted threats, and unexercised authority,
by bringing parents into contempt and rulers into
disregard, breeds rebellion and anarchy in families
and states. But whilst we may speculate thus upon
what would have been the probable consequence of
such a proceeding on the part of God, be it remembered we are all along arguing upon an *impossi-
bility;* "God is not a man that he should lie, or
the Son of man that he should repent." Such is
the immutability of his counsel, and the inviola-
bility of his oath, that he says, " Heaven and
earth shall pass away, but *my word* shall never
pass away;" and it is to show how these apparently irreconcilable things, " mercy and truth,
could meet together, righteousness and peace could
kiss each other," that he has given commandment
to his apostles and prophets to declare unto us
" how he could be just, and the justifier of them
that believe on Jesus;" and how it is that " we,
who were afar off, are made nigh by the blood of

Jesus," so that no moral injury should ensue to
man by his clemency, and no sinner be embol-
dened to sin by his mercy. We are told, that not
one jot or one tittle was to pass from the law till
all was fulfilled ; till then man remained under its
curse, which said, " Cursed is every man that con--
tinueth not in all things written in the book of the
law to do them ;" that no mere man could so perfectly
fulfil this law, as to avoid its penalty or to procure
its repeal, is evident, for every human being came
into the world with one link of the chain broken by
his first father, which, so far from any having it in
his power to repair even by his subsequent conduct,
each man, by superadding his own transgressions,
as we have seen, only widened still more the breach
between man and God.

   " Our Lord Jesus Christ, the Son of God, who
was God and man," uniting in his person the divine and human nature, was alone able to accomplish it ; and to prove that " Day's man," whom Job
longed for, " who could lay his hand upon them
both," and standing between man and his Maker,
as " the repairer of breaches," could fasten on
again the link which connected the human race
with heaven ; not by abrogating the law which
formed the hindrance to it, nor by declaring the
obedience of its commandments unnecessary, but
by fulfilling the stipulated conditions on which its

repeal, as a means of life for man, hung, depriving
it of its condemnatory sentence against him, and
restoring it to him, as that "perfect law of liberty," which could *now* "be written, not with
ink, but with the Spirit of the living God, not in
tables of stone, but in the fleshly tables of the
heart, known and read of all men," (in the holy
lives of his spiritually begotten children,) as *His*
work. He "who came not to *destroy* but to *fulfil*
the law," "magnified it, and made it honourable;"
for thus, He saith, "it becometh us to fulfil all
righteousness." The fulfilment of it by any other
being than *man*, would have been unavailing to
him, as it was ordained *for man alone:* was framed
for them "by angels in the hand of a Mediator,"
and "the seed of the woman could alone perform
the promise made to her, that one of her descendants should avenge her wrongs by visiting condign
punishment upon her enemy the serpent, who had
deceived her to her ruin: "Forasmuch then as
children are *partakers of flesh and blood*, (none
can claim *true* relationship on any other grounds,)
He also himself likewise *took part of the same*,"
that he might thus testify to his identity of interests,
and lawful concernment with the affairs of the
flesh he came to redeem, become answerable for its
debts, and put in his claim for all the benefits ac-
cruing to it, from *His* merits in so doing. "For

this purpose the Son of God was manifested, that
he might destroy the works of the devil." It would
have been no explanation to us of the *cause* of
Adam's fall, and no condemnation, to our apprehension, of his sin, had our Lord taken upon Him
the nature of angels ; for a stronger and superior
nature conquering, where a weaker one was
worsted in the conflict, was to be expected in the
nature of things ; and as they owed no obligations
to man's law, *their* obedience to it, by not di-
minishing *his* debt to it, conveyed no benefit to
him ; " but verily He took not on him the nature
of angels, but took on him the seed of Abraham," to whom there had been a renewal of the
promise, " that in his seed all the nations of the
earth should be blessed ;" and He who, as God, "all
the angels of God worshipped," was made a little
lower than the angels, for the suffering of death,
that He, by the grace of God, should taste death
for every man." " And when the fulness of time
was come, God sent his Son, made of a woman,
made under the law, to redeem them that were
under the law," by coming into the very same nature that the first head wore, and into the very
same circumstances, that he might meet man's
enemies in the same terms, and on the same field
that Adam came by his fall, he might gain the victory. He too encountered the enemy in single

combat, who exhausted the force of all his weapons, hitherto so successfully used against him,
"the lust of the flesh, the lust of the eye, and the
pride of life," and bruised his head, when he
"beheld Satan like lightning fall from heaven,"
whilst yet, according to the prediction announced
to our first parents, his own heel was bruised in
the struggle, and Satan was permitted to go the
whole length of his vengeance in cutting him off
out of the land of the living, who was *bruised* thus
for our iniquities. Had our Lord achieved the
victory, either, in the power of the godhead, His
doing so would have reflected no blame upon
Adam's failure, and could have formed no proper
example for *us* to follow; for as *that* power never
was Adam's, it was no disgrace to him that one
endued with it overcame where he was vanquished
who had it not; and as this power never, either,
could be ours, the call for us to walk in Christ's
steps, when destitute of the means which enabled
him so to walk, would have been a call as unreasonable, I speak it with all humility, on the
part of our God to make, as it would have been
impossible for us to comply with; therefore it is
necessary for us to have a just notion on this
subject, before we can fitly understand our obligation to redemption, and the benefits that have re-
sulted therefrom. We may plainly observe, if we

carefully remark the whole tone and tenour of our
Lord's discourses, and the whole principle of his
actions, that when " He was made man," He re-
nounced, for the time, His omnipotent power, His
omniscient prescience, and omnipresent ubiquity;
laid it aside, and, as it were, put it in abeyance,
and submitted voluntarily to have his power, both
of mind and body, confined within a definite boun-
dary, and circumscribed by certain limits; and,
during his life and walk on earth, he ever spake
and acted as one using not the power of the
eternal Divinity, or exerting the strength of the
divine majesty inherent in him, but as one receiving, as a dependent, the derived aid of the
Holy Ghost, "which was not *given* by measure
unto Him," "who was full of grace and truth," declaring always, he was one "whom the Father *had
sanctified*, and sent into the world," (John x.
36,) whose power was conferred on him by
God for a special purpose. " Thou hast *given Him*
power over all flesh." " Thine they were, and thou
gavest them me." (John xvii. 2, 6.) We are
also told by the apostle, " Christ glorified not
himself to be made priest, but He that said unto
Him, Thou art my Son, to-day have I begotten Thee ;" (Heb. v. 5 ;) " *Called of God* an high
priest after the order of Melchisedec; (ver. 10 ;)
" Whom He *hath appointed* heir of all things,"

(i. 2,) and that " *God anointed* Jesus of Nazareth with the Holy Ghost, and with power, who went about it doing good, for *God was with him.*" (Acts x. 38.) And we are also expressly informed that "*through the Eternal Spirit* He offered himself without spot to God; (Heb. ix. 14.)

And in accordance with these declarations, which give us the key to the whole mystery, we may see that our Lord ran his earthly race below, as one in the dependent spirit of a recipient, not using his own power, as God, to overcome difficulties and perform his duties, but as one who had emptied himself of this power for a time, or suspended its actions; and He, who, as God, " thought it not robbery to be equal with God," " for he *was* God ;" (John i. 1; Phil. ii. 6 ;) yet for a time, and for a purpose of inexpressible mercy and kindness to us, " took upon Him the form of a servant," one under the will, and subject to the authority of a master, even man's divine master, God; and " was made in the likeness of man," taking upon Him 'man's debt, thus of implicit obedience to their law—a debt which, till it was paid by one *in the flesh* he came to redeem, doomed all the race to death. " The sting of death is sin, and the strength of sin is the law," that broken law, that laid hold of every mortal man, as a transgressor of its commands, but Christ deprived it of its sting by satisfying its demands in full; He paid our debt to the uttermost farthing, "who did *no sin*, neither was guile found in His mouth," when he said, "Lo, I come to do thy will, O God," for I am utterly purposed my mouth shall not offend; which will was fulfilled by Him, not through an effort of *divine* power, but in the meek spirit of docile obedience and filial compliance. "Though He were a Son, yet learned He obedience by the things which He suffered, who in the days of His flesh, when He had offered up prayers and supplication, with strong crying and tears, unto Him who was able *to save* Him from death, was heard in that he feared." He was heard, inasmuch as the worst *consequences* of death were averted from *Him*, "whose soul was not left in Hades, neither did His flesh see corruption." Thus "being found in fashion as a man, he humbled himself and became obedient unto death, even the death upon the cross," that "by means of death for the redemption of the transgressions that were under the first Testament, we that are called might receive the promise of eternal inheritance." And the whole life of our Lord was in perfect accordance with this avowed design of letting men see what was "this perfect, and holy, and acceptable will of God;" for except when, upon certain occasions, he let his essential glory and

majesty shine out before the eyes of men, to intimate to them the presence of incarnate Deity,
"Immanuel, God with us," and that continual
exercise of His superhuman powers for the benefit of others to testify He *was* the Messiah, of
whom it was predicted " The Spirit of the Lord is
upon me, because the Lord *hath anointed* me to
preach good tidings to the meek, to bind up the
broken-hearted," &c., and Himself took our infirmities and bare our sicknesses ;" he lived, as far as
regarded *himself*, a life of as implicit dependence
upon the providence of God as the very creatures
of His hand around Him, and refused to assert
His divine prerogatives and power, when urged to
do so by Satan, or solicited to do so by the Jews
who longed for Him thus to attest visibly His
messiahship, yet saying He did so from no incapacity to perform it, but that He refrained for a
time, till certain ends were accomplished for our
salvation, by His relinquishment of it, when He
always foretold, He would resume His dormant
might in unimpaired, nay augmented splendour.

We must observe, then, that our Lord continually
varies his manner of speaking of himself, and his
method of acting, sometimes doing so as " Son of
God," and as frequently as " the Son of man."
Thus, when speaking of his Godhead, he asserts,
"I and my Father *are one.*" " He that hath seen

I 2

me, hath seen the Fathe." Yet, when speaking of himself as man, he says, alluding to his present limited powers, and confined sphere of action, " The Son can do nothing of himself but what he seeth the Father do." "The words that I speak unto you, I speak not of *myself,* but the Father that dwelleth in me, he doeth the works." Again, speaking as God, he saith, " Before Abraham was, I am." Yet speaking as man, he saith, " Of that day and that hour knoweth no man, no not the Son, but the Father." In his actions we must see the same remarkable difference is observable: at one time he feeds five thousand people by a miraculous increase of provisions, yet refuses at another to satisfy the cravings of his own appetite, lest, through the subtlety of the enemy, who would persuade him to exert his divine power to extricate himself out of the first difficulties which presented themselves, he should be foiled thus in his task of conquering in the very same nature over which Satan had formerly gained the victory. We see him again heal in a moment the ear of the high priest's servant which Peter in his too fervent zeal had cut off, yet refuse to deliver himself out of the hands of his enemies; "For how then," he says, "should the Scripture be fulfilled," that he was to be " led as a lamb to the slaughter,"for our sins ? Submitting, too, at one time, to let angels minister to his necessities, and accepting the soothing aid of one, in his agony in the garden, yet refusing to call to his assistance whole legions of them that were at his command, lest this should frustrate his grand design for our salvation; and He, who, as "the resurrection and the life," loosed the bands which held Lazarus in the grave, yet resigned his own body without a struggle, into "those wicked hands which crucified the Lord of glory;" whilst, at the same time, declaring that "no men took this life from him, for that he laid it down of himself, as he had power to lay it down, and he had power to take it up;" to let us plainly understand, that it was neither through weakness, nor yet by compulsion, but of his own free will and choice, that "he died for our sins, according to the Scriptures."

These very marked and explicit declarations, that Christ is both God and man," equal to the Father, as touching his Godhead, but inferior to the Father as touching his manhood," as that pillar and ground of all sound orthodoxy, the Athanasian Creed, expresses it, in place of having been used for our edification and advantage, as God graciously intended it should be in revealing it to us,—have, on the contrary, as we all know, given rise to two very opposite heresies, which have rent the church from the apostles' days until now, with divisions; for " there must be heresies, that they which are approved may be made manifest." Weak, careless, and presumptuous minds, which can look only at one side of a subject, or refuse to receive any truth which the small plumb-line of human intellect cannot fathom, after a superficial examination of the subject, lay hold of a few of the truths which prove one part of the doctrine, and discard all those which relate to the other, and get rid of the difficulty of *reconciling* Scripture by plunging into the yet more fearful one of separating those things which God hath joined together. How wide, nay, and how widely *spreading*, is the awful heresy of the denial of our Lord's divinity, few require to be warned of : but the denial of his humanity is much more prevalent than people imagine, which is *equally Antichrist*, as St. John tells us, (1 John iv. 2, 3 ; 2 John vii.;) though, from being a more insidious, it is a more unsuspected evil. The increasing aversion to the Athanasian Creed may be taken as the pulse of society on this subject, as the proverb that was extant in the days of Jerome seems equally applicable *now :* "Athanasius against all the world, and all the world against Athanasius ;" and *this land* that was honoured *then*, as it has been often since, in giving her attestation to the holy truths he then earnestly contended for, in ceasing to be a *Protestant* one any longer against Rome's errors, seems to be permitted to depart yet further from the faith in all sound doctrine and godliness. Should England, with all her weak concessions to popular clamour, submit to have this glorious creed of the primitive church removed from her ritual, her bulwark is gone, *Ichabod* may be written upon her door, for the glory *is* departed! Any son of *her* communion, who can object or refuse to set the seal of his Amen to the truths contained in it—" that our Lord Jesus Christ, the Son of God, is God and man, God of the substance of his Father, begotten before the world ; and man of the substance of his mother born into the world, *perfect God, and perfect man*, of a reasonable soul and human flesh subsisting,"—must be infected with one or the other of these heresies, both of which this strikes at the root of, and may do well to look to himself, and see how little title he has to enrol himself among *her* members, who has told us all, " which faith unless we keep whole and undefiled, we cannot be saved ;" nay, would do well to listen to still *higher* authority, the word of God himself, which tells him, " such an one" as he, " is subverted," he is departed from the faith, and is worse than an infidel!" But we are addressing those " who hold the faith in unity of spirit, in the bond of peace, and in righteousness of life." And we now come to observe, that as " God and man is one Christ," therefore is He called in Scripture " *the faithful* witness." (Rev. i. 5.)

For He alone, representing in His own person both
parties, can testify truly to each of the other; " for
a mediator is not a mediator of one," (Gal. iii. 20,)
but a person who steps in between two parties for
the purpose of reconciliation of differences; and, it
stands to reason, must therefore be one possessed
of very peculiar qualities to fit him for the office,
and enable him to obtain the confidence of both.
But in this most delicate case the difficulties appeared almost insurmountable, seeing the difference
existed between the High and Holy One which inhabiteth eternity, and man, a poor worm of the
earth.

Were we to go through the whole circle of created
intelligence we had ever heard of, or fancied in
existence, we should yet feel they were all as little
able, as they would probably have been inclined, to
stand in the gap for us. Had our Lord Jesus Christ
been only one of them, or had he been man *only*,
He had had neither dignity nor authority to undertake the task; or, being made man, had he ever
" sinned after the similitude of Adam's transgression," or of that of any of his descendants; as being
then himself numbered with the party that had
offended, he had been utterly disqualified for the
office; for the conditions on which any one was to
ascend into the hill of the Lord, or rise up in His
holy place," were, " he shall have clean hands and

a pure heart that hath not lifted up itself into vanity, nor sworn to deceive his neighbour, for " to the clean thou wilt show thyself clean."

Had Christ been God only, as being the aggrieved party, it was not to be expected his sympathies could be on the side of the aggressors ; nor would any man have dared to put his cause into His hands, seeing He was the person whose honour was concerned in his destruction, whom all men knew to be a consuming fire to *sin*." Had He been man only, he never could have testified truly to man of God, " for no man hath seen God at any time," " whom no man hath seen or can see ;" but, " being the only begotten Son which was in the bosom of the Father, he hath declared him, " for the word was made flesh, and dwelt among us, and we beheld his glory, the glory as of the only begotten of the Father ; and by Him " the light was manifested and made light," made intelligible to our finite minds, for we should have been " blasted with excess of light," had it not been thus veiled in human flesh, and so softened and brought down to our weak apprehension, in the person of the Messiah ; and thus, " we all beholding, as in a glass, the glory of the Lord Christ, who is the image of God, hath shined in our hearts, to give the light of the knowledge of the glory of God, in the face of Christ Jesus."

And thus is fulfilled to us the prayer of
Moses—" I beseech thee show me thy glory,"
which many prophets and righteous men besides
desired to see, and did not see; how, in the person
of the God-man, all the seemingly conflicting attributes of God had met together, like the varied
prismatic rays which all merge into the *one* pure
light of *love*. " Mercy and Truth had indeed met
together," for " Truth had at last sprung out of
the *earth*," in " the root out of a dry ground," "the
rod out of the stem of Jesse, and the branch out
of His roots;" and " righteousness had looked down
from heaven,* saying, " This is my beloved Son, in
whom I am well pleased; hear ye Him." Had our
Lord been God either, only, he never could have
borne a "*faithful* witness" for *us* " in things per-
taining to God; but now, " knowing that we have
not an high priest that cannot be touched with the
feeling of our infirmities, but was in all points

---

* The truth of God's promise is in earth to man declared,
or from the earth is the everlasting verity, God's son, risen to
life, and the true righteousness of the Holy Ghost looking out
of heaven, and in most liberal largess dealt upon all the world.
Thus is glory and praise *rebounded upwards* to God above,
for His mercy and truth; and thus is peace *come down* from
heaven to men of good and faithful heart. Thus is " mercy
and truth," as David writeth, " together met; thus is peace
and righteousness embracing and kissing each other."—*Homily
on the Resurrection of our Saviour Jesus Christ.*

tempted like as we are," we may come boldly to the
throne of grace, where we have " a merciful and
faithful High Priest to make reconciliation for iniquity," and " who can have compassion on the ignorant, and them that are out of the way ;" and if
any man sin, he may say, " Plead thou my cause,
O Lord," for " we have *an advocate* with the Father,
Jesus Christ the righteous, into whose hands, at
the hour of death too, we may commend our Spirits,
saying, " Thou hast redeemed us, O Lord, thou God
of truth."

In one more striking particular yet, we must contemplate this interesting and important subject.
By one man " sin entered into the world, and death
passed upon all men, for that all have sinned," in
the person of their head and representative, who
were all (as Levi was in the loins of Abraham,
Heb. vii. 10) enclosed in their first father and
head, therefore, " over all," even to the innocent
babe that " had done neither good nor evil,"
" death *reigned* by one," (as it is expressively described,) the King of Terrors no mortal man could
either avert or subdue.   It might have been deemed
satisfaction enough to the justice of God, for any
thing we *know* to the contrary, had men thus drunk
to the dregs the cup of physical and spiritual ills
his own sin had brought upon him ; it might have been
deemed expiation enough for his offence, and might
have wiped it, as well as his name, for ever from the

book of God's remembrance ; but, even supposing
this hypothesis to be true, its doing so brought no
benefit to man, though an atonement, which com-
pleted his soul's ruin, *might* have brought glory to
God ; any more, in fact, than the convicted felon
derives from expiating *his* crime on the gallows.
He would have passed into Death's dark prison-
house to come forth no more, except to receive his
sentence for transference to a still more fearful
punishment, in that " *outer* darkness, where shall
be weeping and gnashing of teeth."

But let it be even supposed, that any one of the
human race *could* so perfectly have fulfilled the
law, as in any way to have washed out the original
stain, cancelled his own debt, and so countermanded
the sentence against him that had gone out, and had
been able to put forth his hand in consequence and
take of the tree of life, and eat and live for ever,
which we have clearly shown to be a thing utterly
impossible for any man to do; still, his doing so even,
could have benefited *himself alone*, his own merits
would have sufficed *only* for his own wants, and left
him no superfluity to be an available fund for *others* ;
for Scripture tells us, " though *three* such men as
Noah, Daniel, and Job, stood before God, they
could deliver neither son nor daughter, they should
deliver but their own souls by their righteousness ;"
" for no man *can* deliver his brother, nor make
agreement unto God for him, for it cost more to

redeem their souls, so that he must let that alone for ever, for the redemption of their souls is precious," and far above any price that poor, polluted human nature can pay for it; and the doctrine of supererogatory works, which has so prominent a place in the Church of Rome, is utterly repudiated by the Bible as a falsehood ; for man, it is shown us *there*, has disqualified himself by his sinfulness for either being a saviour to himself or for others.

Had our only Lord and Saviour Jesus Christ, then, *been man only*, *His* attempting our salvation would have been as ineffectual for " redeeming our souls from the power of the grave," and rescuing our bodies from its mansion of corruption, as the sacrifices under the law had proved. Had He entered the tomb merely as one paying, by death, the forfeit of his own transgression, as a breaker of God's law, he was thus legally in the hands of "him who had the power of death, even the devil," who would have secured him for ever as his *rightful* prey ; and if so, and if Christ had *not* been raised from the dead, we should be yet in our sins, and all of those who fell asleep in Jesus, perished as certainly as those who died in ignorance or disbelief of a Saviour !

But though our blessed Lord, glory be to His holy name ! did indeed enter those dismal precincts, as all human flesh entered them, (for he descended

into hell, Hades,) bound hand and foot, and tied
about with grave-clothes, in the custody of man's
relentless foe,—*the triumph ended there !* for "the
Prince of this world came, and found nothing in
him," "the Lamb without blemish and without
spot," that afforded a legal title for his detention ;
"*therefore,*" says He, "did my heart rejoice, and
my flesh rest in hope, because thou wilt not leave
my soul in hell, neither wilt thou suffer my flesh to
see corruption." "Whom God therefore raised
from the dead, having loosed the pains of death, for
it was not *possible he* should be *holden* of them,"
who was, in his own person "the Prince of Life !"
Our divine head, and brother in the flesh, condescended thus to humble himself unto death, that
into the citadel where Satan's strength lay, he
might penetrate ; *there* He met our mortal foe face
to face, and though the *particulars* of that final encounter are hid from us, the *effects* and *fruits* of it
were gloriously revealed, and the victory of our
Lord fully manifested, when, "the third day He
rose again from the dead," He emerged triumphant
from the tomb as conqueror, "the Captain of our
salvation" made perfect through sufferings, having
"taken the prey from the spoiler, and delivered the
lawful captive ;" nay, "having taken *him* captive
whose captives we were," "having abolished death,
and brought life and immortality to light through

the Gospel," and having obtained " the keys of hell
and of the grave," he rolled back the stone that
would have lain for ever on man's imprisoned body,
fulfilling the word that was spoken of Him, " He
will destroy in this mountain the face of the cover-
ing over all people, and the veil that is spread over
all nations he will swallow up in *death* in *victory*,"
and affording us a pledge of the completion of
it; " Thy dead men shall live, together (with)
my dead body shall they arise. Awake and
sing, ye that dwell in dust; for thy dew is as
the dew of herbs, and the earth shall cast forth
her dead, when all that are in their graves shall
hear his voice, and shall come forth, some to everlasting life, and some to shame and everlasting contempt ;" and giving the believer this day-star of
hope in his breast, to guide him through the dark
valley of the shadow of death, that though they all
must, like their divine Master, pass " through the
grave and gate of death," they need fear no evil, for

" Their Saviour has passed through its portals before them,
And the lamp of his love is their guide through the tomb."

HEBER.

Thus "we see Jesus, for the suffering of death,
crowned with glory and honour ;" and being made
perfect, he became *the author* of eternal life to
all them that obey Him :" for we come now to the
practical part of our subject, our Lord renouncing,

as altogether unbecoming in man, that proud
spirit of independence of God, (the assumption of which had been Adam's ruin,) while He
wore man's nature, acted and spake ever, we see,
as one who stood not in His own strength, but
declared, "I can do nothing *of myself*, but as the
Father hath taught me I speak these things," and
saying, He sought not honour *himself*, but *His*
glory alone who "sent him," (John vii. 16—18 ;)
in all this, giving us an insight into the exceeding
sinfulness of Adam's sin, and the cause of his fall;
who, aspiring to be as God, lost his high standing
even as man, and put himself under the yoke of
Satan, who had laid the glittering bait before him;
and an insght, moreover, into the sin of our
own hearts, as well as instructs us in our own duties.
For not only did Adam fall by admitting the entrance
of this principle of all evil into his mind, but we
may, if we have any knowledge of our own hearts,
ascertain that this is *still* the root of bitterness
within us, which brings forth fruit unto death, the
seed of corruption sown in our hearts by the fall,
which is incapable of producing anything but
weeds.

. Our Lord, in declaring the grand principle of the
Gospel to a master of Israel, repeated three times
over, to mark its importance, "We must be born
again," "be born of the Spirit," ere we can see the

kingdom of God ; and the meaning of this is evident, when we see our state by *nature* is ever fitly described as a state of *death*, and therefore does St. Paul describe us " as *dead* in trespasses and sins." How total and how complete this destruction of the vital principle within us became by the fall, we can best learn by observing the terms used to describe our recovery from it, as, had the injury been trivial or partial, such strong and compendious terms would have been most inappropriate ; for unless there had been an *entire* loss of the principle of life, there could have been no necessity for our being *regenerated*, or born again, as are the terms used by our Lord, and St. Paul, St. James, St. Peter, and St. John. (Rom. viii. 11, John iii. and 1 John v. 1, James i. 18, 1 Peter i. 3, 23.)

Our having to " be renewed after the image of him who had created us," testifies how wholly all traces of the Divine likeness were lost, in which we were *originally* made, or the necessity for our being recast in that divine mould would not have existed ; our having to " put on the new man," which after God *is created* (the term is a very remarkable one) in righteousness and true holiness ;" " for we are his workmanship, *created* in Christ Jesus unto good works,"—may convince us how entirely dead the old principle of life within us had become, to give occa-

sion for a new act of God's divine creative power
to restore it to us. Our having to pass from death
unto life denotes a change as far beyond the *natural*
powers of man to accomplish, as it is for a corpse to
reanimate itself, or a dry stick to enkindle itself
with fire. Our having to "pass from darkness into
light," from "blindness unto recovery of sight,"
to be "*transformed*" so completely as that " old
things must pass away, and *all things* become *new,*"
"the heart of stone to be taken away, and to be replaced by a heart of flesh :"—all these expressive
figures and strong terms prove to us, not only that
we were fallen creatures, but that we had also entirely lost the power of self-recovery, and of re-
instating ourselves in our former condition ; being
cut off from the conduit, which conveyed life to
our souls.

"The first Adam was made a living soul," but,
being unfaithful to his trust, he lost that which was
committed to his keeping, and so transmitted a
body of sin and death to all his descendants. " The
last Adam was made a *quickening* spirit," to *restore
to us* the life He had thus lost ; and He, our Lord
Jesus, having faithfully discharged *His* trust,
"therefore hath the Father given him to *have life in
himself*, that he might give eternal life to all that
believe in him." For we must understand that the

resurrection of Jesus *as* intimately affects all the race, by reason of our federal and fleshly union, with him, as the death of Adam has done.

Unless we thus see the oneness of the nature and the sameness of the flesh in the two heads, both in the fall and in the redemption, it is impossible for us to comprehend *why*, " through the fault of one, many thus be dead," and *why*, " through the righteousness of one, many are thus made alive." Till we see that the figure of the head and the members, so often referred to in the Bible, &c., and fully illustrated in 1 Cor. xii., Eph. iv., Col. ii. &c., is a *real thing*, given us to show our actual connexion with the one who ruined, and the one who restored our race again, we shall have very inadequate ideas of the misfortune which befel us in the fall, and the blessings and benefits flowing to us through redemption; and that, through our union thus with our first Head, we, who were all contained in this one germ or seed of the nature, fell with Him; and in the latter case, we, whose existence was equally bound up with that of our second Head, were, by His fulfilment of the terms of life, and perfect obedience, restored again to our forfeited privileges: for, as Barnard of Clairvaux says, " it was *man* that owed, it was *man* that paid, because the head and the body *are Christ;* the head satisfied for its own members, Christ for His own bowels;

therefore " for this cause I sanctify myself, that *they also* may be sanctified through the truth ;" and, as the apostle says, " both he that sanctifieth and they that are sanctified are all of *one*, for which cause he is not ashamed to call them brethren ; "for if the first fruit be holy, the lump also is holy," and if the root be holy, so are the branches. Therefore do we see what a significant figure was the waving of the primal sheaf of the Israelitish corn, which consecrated the *whole* harvest!

One of the same human nature, one of the flesh, had at length complied with the conditions, to which were appended the readmission of *the race* to the Divine presence ; he had been able to present himself to God, with " the clean hands and the pure heart" God demanded. Yea, one "made of a woman, made under the law," had so entirely fulfilled the will of God, as to be able to approach God on the terms of His own appointment, and to lay claim to the promise, "He shall receive the blessing from the Lord, and righteousness from the God of his salvation ;" therefore to Him was it said, " Thou hast loved righteousness and hated iniquity, therefore God, even thy God, hath anointed thee with the oil of gladness above thy fellows." And " like the precious ointment upon the head, that ran down upon the beard, even unto Aaron's beard, that went down to the skirts of his garment ;" so did the blessing include all the members of Christ's mystical body, and extended to them all, "by the which will we are sanctified through the offering of the body of Jesus once for all," who had paid God the debt of full obedience to his law we owed, and paid, in His person, the whole penalty of our transgression when he made his soul an offering for sin. And He that descended thus into the lower parts of the earth, ascended also up far above all heavens, that He might fill all things, and receive gifts for men, even for his enemies, that the Lord God might dwell among them. "Wherefore God hath also highly exalted Him," and being by the right hand of God exalted, He received from the Father the promise of the Holy Ghost, and for it was now become a perfectly righteous and consistent thing with God, seeing that *the nature* and the whole race were thus consecrated afresh by the atonement of His Son, to return, as He says, and be a Father unto us, and to set apart each believer's heart as a temple "where prayer should be set forth in his sight as the incense, and lifting up of their hands as an evening sacrifice." For "now is Christ risen from the dead, and become the first fruits of them that slept;" "for except a corn of wheat die, it abideth alone, but if it die, it bringeth forth much fruit." For this reason did our Lord say, "It is expedient for you that I go away; for, if I go not away, the Comforter will not

come unto you ; but if I depart, I will send him
unto you ;" "for I am come that ye may have life,
and that ye may have it more abundantly." Which
promises were *visibly* and gloriously fulfilled, when,
at the day of Pentecost, the first full effusion of
it proclaimed itself, like cloven tongues of fire upon
the apostles' heads, and in the miraculous gifts, as
well as increase of spiritual grace, which it conferred upon them ; and is *still* as fully, though more
imperceptibly, fulfilled in the case of each believer
who is brought out of death into life by its influ-
ences, and " Christ is formed in them the hope of
glory," "whose lives are hid with Christ in God ;"
and that kingdom of God " which cometh not with
observation," is erected in their souls, and *He* reigns
in peace and righteousness, who, when he shall
appear, then shall they also appear with him in
glory.   So far, in fact, from Christ having done and
suffered these things to excuse our doing so, He did
it, we may judge from this, for the very purpose of
procuring the means for enabling us to present our
bodies "a living sacrifice, holy and acceptable in
God's sight, which is our *reasonable* service." For it
is *now* surely a very *reasonable* and just demand on
the part of our Maker, and not like that of the
Egyptian taskmaster, " to make bricks without
straw," when he has replenished us with a full
provision for its accomplishment, to exact of us to be

' Holy as He which hath called us is holy ;" for as He has given Christ to be not only " a leader and commander to the people," but a new fountain of life to them, constituting Him the head, to be a channel of communicating it once more to them, (for the head was raised up thus, that life might from it flow down into all the members who might " live through Him,") we having the very same Spirit granted unto us, for " the manifestation of the Spirit *is given* to *every man* to profit withal," (1 Cor. xii. 4, 13,) God, who hath thus richly supplied us with the means of obeying it, may well now bid each of us " walk even as Christ walked," " who has left us an example that we should *follow* His steps ;" which, according to the degree our finite powers admit of, and according to the measure of the Spirit which is apportioned to us, it is now become practicable for us to do, seeing we are " *made partakers of the Divine nature.*" And "if the Spirit of Him that raised up Christ from the dead, dwell in us, He that raised up Jesus from the dead shall also quicken our mortal bodies by His Spirit that dwelleth in us ;" for " we are made," truly, " partakers of Christ" in believing ; inasmuch as, in the person of our Surety and Representative, *we* died for our sins, when *He* died *for us ;* and in His person we also *arose* when He arose, as justified persons, who had expiated our offence, and were

free henceforward from its condemnation. " For as
many of us," says the apostle, " as were baptized
into Jesus Christ, were baptized into his death,
that like as Christ was raised from the dead, we
also should walk in newness of life."

We must, therefore, be born of the Spirit ere we
can bring forth the fruits of the Spirit, for " it is
the Spirit that *quickeneth*, the flesh profiteth nothing."
It may indeed gain us a name on *earth*, and a high
place in the esteem and affections of our fellow men,
and may enable us to do much that is creditable and
respectable below ; but these, its fruits and effects,
cannot accompany us to heaven, or find any acceptance in God's sight : the fruits of the Spirit we
alone can carry with us *there ;* for " blessed are the
dead that die *in the Lord* from henceforth ; yea,
saith the Spirit, that they may rest from their
labours, and their works do follow them." As
every tree " brings forth fruit of its kind," and a
brier cannot bear figs, therefore must we be grafted
into the true vine, that we may bring forth fruit
unto true holiness. " The works of the flesh are
manifest," says the apostle, who gives a sad list of
them ; they are indeed " corrupt according to the
deceitful lusts :" but the fruits of the Spirit are
love, joy, peace, long-suffering, &c., and they that
are Christ's have crucified the flesh with its affections and lusts, and are renewed in the spirit of

their minds." And this spirit we receive, " not through the righteousness of the law, but *through the hearing of faith ;*" for, as we have shown, that which no merits, and no attempts, and no endeavours of our own ever could have procured for us, Christ our Lord hath obtained, to whom it is given to have life in himself, where, as in a treasure-house, it is stored up for us ; and this "faith which, obtains it for us, cometh *by hearing,* and hearing *by the word of God.*" (Rom. x. 17.)

When we receive with meekness the engrafted word which is able to save our souls, and " as new born-babes" too, when "we have been begotten again to a lively hope," " we desire the sincere milk of the word, that we may *grow thereby.*" That which *implants* the vital principle, must also *nourish* it ; for, having *begun* in the Spirit, we are not *made perfect* by the flesh," says the apostle, but " grow up unto Him in all things, which is our head," "the author and finisher of our faith ;" and if we " *live* in the Spirit, we do also *walk* in the Spirit," " through the Spirit do mortify the deeds of the body ;" " through the Spirit wait for the hope of righteousness which is by faith, and " of the Spirit reap everlasting life."

He who has the residue of the Spirit, says, " Ask and ye shall have, seek and ye shall find, knock and it shall be opened unto you ; for every one that asketh receiveth, and he that seeketh findeth, and to him

that knocketh it shall be opened." "If a son ask
bread of any of you that is a father, will he give him
a stone ? And if he ask him for a fish, will he for a
fish give him a serpent? or if he shall ask an egg,
will he offer him a scorpion? If ye then, being
evil, know how to give good gifts unto your children,
how much more shall your heavenly Father give
the Holy Spirit to them *that ask him ?*" "Wherefore it saith, Awake thou that sleepest, and arise
from the dead, and Christ shall give thee light ;" for
to be carnally minded *is death,* but to be spiritually
minded *is life* and peace.

If there are any who are conscious they do not possess
" the new heart and the right spirit," or that having
" tasted of the heavenly gift," they have so quenched
and grieved it, that it has departed from them, we are
not left without instruction or example as to what it is
our proper course to pursue, or what to do to obtain
it ; for the prayers of God's saints are left on
record in the book of inspiration, as if purposely to
show us we must "*take with us* words, and turn to
the Lord, and say to Him, Take away all iniquity,
and receive us graciously : so will we render the
calves (the sacrifices) of our lips," Hosea xiv. 1.
And the 51st and many other Psalms show us
what are the words proper to take with us to God,
and furnish us with them. "Create in me a new
heart, O God, and renew a right spirit within me,"

" *Quicken me,* O Lord, according to thy loving-kindness." (cxix. verse 159.) "Quicken me, O Lord,
according to thy judgments." (verse 156.) "My soul
cleaveth to the dust, quicken thou me according to
thy word." So that we are both shown what it is
our duty to do in these sad circumstances, are
forbid to despond or be idle, but both encouraged
and expressly taught to approach to God, and in
what manner to approach Him, "who will be sanctified in all them that draw near to him."

CHAPTER VI.

WE may then very evidently perceive, that though
our argument has brought us to this important conclusion, that " in Christ we *have* redemption
through His blood, the forgiveness of sins, " it is by
no means intended that we should stop here, any
more than we should expect the traveller to do,
who had received his passport and provisions for
the way ; for it is, in fact, at this point that the very
journey to heaven by the Christian commences :
and so far from pardon being regarded as the grand
end of his desires, it is to be regarded only as a
means to a much higher end. " Forasmuch, then, as
Christ hath suffered for us in the flesh, arm yourselves with the same mind ; for he that hath suffered
in the flesh hath ceased from sin, that he should

live the rest of his time no longer to the lusts of
man, but to the will of God;" and "if ye then be
risen with Christ, seek those things which are above,
where Christ sitteth on the right hand of God."
The believer being relieved from the irksome
bondage of working *for* life, and from the miserable
uncertainty us to whether God was regarding him
with an eye of favour or a frown of wrath, works
naturally now, and joyfully, *from* life, being free
to turn to his duties with an easy mind, when he is
at rest on that anxious question, " What shall I do
to be saved ?" and so speaks, and so acts, as one
that shall be " judged by the perfect law of liberty ;"
for " I will run the way of thy commandments,
when thou hast set my heart at liberty," says the
Psalmist, who felt that till his feet, which were tied
and bound with the chain of his sins, were loosed
from their fetters, not one step onwards could he
take in the strait and narrow path which alone
leadeth to everlasting life ; not one deed could he
perform acceptably to Him, " whose service is a
service of perfect freedom." But as the duty and
service *God* requires is so very different from any
that men can exact from his fellow men below, it is
necessary to enter more fully into the subject ere we
proceed.

All the work and service below, which man pays

to man, may be discharged without *the heart* taking
any part in it, nay, may be faithfully done, while
yet all its feelings may be opposed to the person
we serve, with the utmost aversion. Self-interest,
want, compulsion, covetousness, or fear, may call
into action, and place at the disposal of our fellow-
creatures, every faculty of the mind, and every
power of the body ; and if these do their parts well,
men may be satisfied, while they remain in perfect ignorance, perhaps, of the feelings of disgust
and dislike which accompanied, and the motive
which prompted, the action. But it is not so with
God, and with the duty He requires of us. He
who made man's heart, and formed it to be within
his breast, as it were, the harp of creation, which
should ever " praise God according to His excellent greatness," keeps his hands upon the strings,
and discovers in a moment every jarring note
which occasions a dissonance in that harmony
which should sound in His ears from its every
movement ; and when He finds no responsive answer to His touch, His language is that of disappointed affection : " I have nourished and brought
up children, and they have rebelled against me:"
" O my people, what have I done unto thee, and
wherein have I wearied thee ? Can a maid forget
her ornaments, and a bride her attire ? Yet my

people have forgotten *me* days without number."
"For the Lord God, whose name is Jealous, is a
jealous God."

There is a wide difference, too, between the work
done for man, and the work done for God, besides,
in this respect, that man stands too much in need
of the assistance of his fellow men to be very
rigorous in his inquiries into the feelings which in-
stigated the performance of his duty, and he
too gladly awards him his wages for services he
cannot dispense with, should he be ever so suspicious of the motive of the person he employs. But
with the Almighty, how opposite is the case! " Can
man be profitable unto God?" " What have we,
that we can render unto Him, that we have not received from Him? Behold, Lebanon is not sufficient to burn, nor the beasts thereof sufficient for
a burnt offering," and " of *thine own* do we give
thee," we must ever admit in all that we render
unto God: and what can *we* do for Him, that He
cannot effect by higher and better agents? nay,
without the interposition of any? He who slew in
one night, in the camp of the Assyrians, by the
hand of a single angel, one hundred fourscore and
five thousand men, stands in no need of the armies
of the earth to avenge himself upon His enemies. He
who could call a world into existence with the word
of His mouth, and swept away its inhabitants by a

flood, is independent of our puny services to effect His purposes; and He who could of the very stones raise up children unto Abraham, or cause them to cry out and sing, did man withhold his tribute of praise due to Him, needs not even our voices to join in the heavenly choir, who rest not day nor night, saying, "Holy, holy, holy is the Lord," though out of the mouths of very babes and sucklings of earth, He condescends to say, praise is perfected in his ears.

It was not because God stood in need of our services below, or required our aid, that He breathed into man's nostrils the breath of life, placed him at his post of duty below, and requires him to give an account of his stewardship at the last day. Man, for his own good and advantage, had the high honour put upon him, that unlike "the horse and mule that had no understanding," but who ate and drank and went the round of their little duties and enjoyments, unconscious of the Author of their existence, "God had given him an understanding that he might know Him that is true," and on his head was placed the crown of glory, that he had a rational mind and immortal soul, capable of a union and communion with the Father of his spirit; and though the Almighty was under no necessity of employing his services to accomplish his designs, yet was He graciously

pleased to accept of his services, to put many
pleasing duties into his hands, and to allow of his
aid in carrying on his plan of mercy below, in
correspondence with purer and higher agents above.

But man, having by his own sin suffered disloca-
tion from this his proper position on earth, soon
prostituted these his natural powers, given him for
this purpose, to lower and baser uses, and, for his
own aggrandisement and interest, to make himself a name upon earth, or to help others to do so,
he engaged in stupendous undertakings, wherein
the glory of his divine Master was not concerned,
nor his will consulted. Pyramids and lofty tem-
ples arose, magnificent and imposing to the sight ;
the arts enriched the earth, and science enlightened
men's minds, till hardly one grand deed seemed
left unaccomplished, one noble enterprise left un-
achieved, whilst yet all this, that was "highly es-
teemed among men, was abomination in the sight
of God," when the only principle *He* can recognise
and bless, "the single eye to his glory," the desire to obey his commands was wanting ; and He
"for whose pleasure men are and were created,"
was left out of account in all their calculations,
and who, therefore, blasted with the breath of his
displeasure every Babel which thus arose, a monument of man's perverseness and apostasy ; and to
show that the wisdom of this world is foolishness

L

with God, when not arising from a right principle,
or not directed to a right end.   And though these
wonderful aspirations of genius, and astonishing per-
formances of physical skill, seemed but a realization
of Satan's promise, "Ye shall be as gods," God
punished the blasphemous pretensions by making
foolish the wisdom of this world,—for it is written,
"I will destroy the wisdom of the wise, and will
bring to nothing the understanding of the prudent,
that no man may glory in man."

The first and great commandment under the
Law, as well as under the *Gospel*, was, "Thou
shalt love the Lord thy God, with all thy heart,
and with all thy soul, and with all thy strength."
(Deut. vi. 5, Matt. xxii. 37, 38.)   For God, as
we have seen, did not require *work*, but *love*; and
however the faculties with which man was at first
endowed, and the circumstances in which he was
at first placed, every way fitted and disposed him
for the sublime duty, enduing him with the feeling of a child to its parent, and of a grateful servant to a kind master, the fall, as we have shown,
subverted all these feelings in his soul, and made
him incapable of rendering it to God.   Having
thrown off the yoke of allegiance to his heavenly
Lord, and placed himself in the position of an
usurper who had seized on the reins himself, he
had instilled into his mind a sense of suspicious

fear and angry defiance of Him that roused his whole heart and soul into a state of rebellion against God, besides making him incapable of giving the due meed of love and thankfulness it was his duty to do.

The sacrifices under the law were instituted to show him there was a way of return to God; and by intimating to him, through these means of God's own providing, the placability of his Maker, and His merciful intentions to restore him to his favour, they would tend to awaken hope in his mind, and give some degree of confidence and ground for affection in his heart; and by the faint light which they afforded, the spirits of just men in those days were made perfect, and through faith and patience inherited the promises; as we see by the glorious constellation of them St. Paul points out to us in the heavenly mansions, in the eleventh of the Hebrews; but the veil was still upon their hearts, and still hung over the entrance to the mercy-seat, leaving in impenetrable obscurity the present feelings and future intentions of God to his church, so as to keep men's hearts at a painful distance from Him.

The law was given not to remove this distance, evidently, or to take away this obstruction, but to show it to us more plainly, to open men's eyes more perfectly to the great separation which sin had

made between them and their God; "for by the
law was the knowledge of sin," by its high requirements was man's sin more fully revealed, for it
placed the standard of holiness so high in man's
sight, as to convince him of the utter hopelessness
of his ever reaching it by his own doings, or gain-
ing the reward of life by its fulfilment. Man, seeing by it the extensive demands of God's will, and
the unflinching strictness of His requirements, must
by this be led to despair of justifying himself by
it, or proving himself innocent of its breach to
his Maker; and thus the law, as St. Paul says,
acted as "our schoolmaster, to bring us to Christ."
It taught us, as we could never obtain God's
forgiveness or merit His favour by our own righteousness, to cast ourselves entirely on His mercy,
and lay hold by faith of the hope set before us in
the Gospel.

Thus "the law entered that the offence might
abound;" that the extent of our offences being,
through its light, made manifest to us, we might
renounce all attempts at going about to establish our own righteousness and be led to submit ourselves to the righteousness of God, (of His
institution,) and so "believe on Jesus, as the end
of the law for righteousness to every one that believeth." "If there *had* been a law given which
could have given life," says the apostle, "verily

righteousness would have been by the law, and
there would then have been no occasion for " the
agony and bloody sweat, the cross and passion, the
precious death and burial," of our only Lord and
Saviour Jesus Christ: man's own obedience would
have rendered this unnecessary ; but man had a
law in his members warring against the law of his
mind, so that he could not do the thing that he
would ; for when he would do good, evil was present
with him, and the good that he would he did not,
and the evil that he would not, that he did.   " But
what the law could not do, in that it was weak
through the flesh, God sending his own Son in the
likeness of sinful flesh," accomplished, that, by virtue of our union with Him, through His indwelling Spirit, " the righteousness of the law might be
fulfilled in us, who walk not after the flesh, but after
the Spirit."

Christ, as is shown in Romans vii., having dis-
solved the union which subsisted between us and
the law of works, which, as long as that union
lasted, kept us in bondage to it; " for a woman
which hath a husband is bound by the law to her
husband as long as he liveth, but if the husband be
dead, she is loosed from the law of her husband ;"
and continuing this very significant figure, St. Paul
says, " Wherefore, my brethren, ye also are become dead to the law by the body of Christ, (that

being dead wherein we are held,) that ye should be married to another, even to Him who is raised from the dead, that we should bring forth fruit unto God." And as many as are led by the Spirit of God, they are the sons of God; wherein, under another equally expressive figure, we are again taught our spiritual relationship to the Father of mercies, "for we have not received the spirit of bondage again to fear;" this is now ejected from our hearts by the "perfect love which casteth out fear, because fear hath torment, and he that feareth is not made perfect in love;" "but we have received the spirit of adoption, whereby we cry, Abba, Father;" being born of God, "born of the Spirit," re-introduces us into this filial confidence and affection; and being children of God through the Spirit, we have the heart of a child to its father once more, for "we have known and believed the love that God hath to us," and love begets love.

And the apostle "whom Jesus loved," hath let us see that not in vain for himself and for us was this glorious distinction conferred upon him, for he had drunk in so largely of the spirit of his divine Master, as to have been enabled to handle the subject in a manner worthy of one who had leaned on the breast of Jesus; and most clearly does he show us that though "God is *love*," and altogether worthy of being loved by his creatures, and every way

calculated to call forth their warmest and their
fondest affections towards Him, yet that this would
have been quite insufficient to have either encouraged or admitted even of an approach to Him,
placed in the circumstances we were with regard
to Him, unless *He* had made the first advances;
for we *did* not, because we *dare* not, love God, till
we knew that God loved us; for says he, "Not
that *we* loved God, but that God loved us, and
sent His Son to be the propitiation for our sins."
"We love Him, *because* He first loved us." We
may venture, nay we feel impelled to do so : love
springs up unbidden in the heart, when we perceive what God has done for us : as it does to all
who endear themselves to us by any act of devotedness to us, or who have made any sacrifices
for our deliverance from danger or rescue from ruin.

He who formed the spirit of man within him
knew how vain it was to exact love as a right, or
enforce it as a duty, when we were so situated as
to render our compliance with the demand imprac-
ticable; for that though we might offer any *other*
service, might "give all our goods to feed the poor,
and give our body to be burned," yet our *love* can
neither be gained by compulsion, nor even given by
us at our will; for it is not a sensation so at our
command, or at the disposal of others, that we *can*
give it at pleasure, or yield it through a threat.

Were we to go to any criminal under sentence of death, and require it authoritatively for the monarch whose law doomed him justly to his fate, or try to excite his admiration for the law which demanded his imprisonment, and the forfeit of his life, we know how vain would be our attempts, as the more we showed him how excellent, and mild, and righteous this king was, the more would he shrink with horror from the idea of having injured one so every way worthy of regard and estimation; and the more we exhibited to him the equity and wisdom of the statutes of the realm, the more would his heart rise up in stubborn indignation and abhorrence of those very excellences which required his destruction, most properly, as an infringer of them; and the very ground which we took to plead for them, only rendered his sin against them more inexcusable, and his sentence inevitable. And thus the sinner, the more he sees that God is very greatly to be loved and adored for His goodness and His righteousness, the more it aggravates the sense of his *own* guilt in having sinned against such a being, and increases the bitterness of his anguish to see how holy, and just, and good, that law is of which he is a transgressor.

And the very perfections of the Divine Being, when he turns to contemplate them as they are all set in array against *him*, only drive him with terror further than ever from His presence; for He feels that it is out of the question his attempting to love his Maker, and thus obey his first command, even should he break his heart in the vain attempt, situated as he is; for the very reason why he *ought* to love God, forms also the very strongest reason why He cannot. Every reflection upon his greatness and his goodness, rendering the sense of his presence now insupportable, and the idea of appearing before him hereafter, intolerable! And nothing short of a principle which can remove all this *just cause* for our dread of God, and reassure our hearts of *his* having provided a way for our recovery, which could satisfy his justice, and testify to *his* righteousness, as well as allow of the exercise of mercy towards us miserable sinners, and could show us the deed was *done* which had accomplished it, and the way open which *admitted* of our approach, could have attracted our hearts again to Him, from whom they seemed for ever divorced.

Our case was desperate; we had so fallen into the lowest depths of hopeless woe, that nothing but a love unfathomable, indescribable, could have restored us; but " when none eye pitied us, and we were cast out to the loathing of our person, and became vain in our imagination, and our foolish heart was darkened, being filled with all unrighteousness, as was our natural condition sketched by

the pen of inspiration, " God *so* loved the world,"
" He passed by us, he looked upon us, and the
time was the time of love," that would have been
the moment of rejection and abhorrence, were the
measure of *his* love to be meted by what we have
ever known of the love of man for man, or what
we had ever conceived of the love felt for man by
his Creator ! " for scarcely for a righteous man
will one die, yet peradventure for a good man
some would even dare to die; but *God* hath com-
mended *his* love to us, in that, while we were sinners, Christ died for the *ungodly*." While we
were rebels in open revolt against the High Majesty of heaven, *none* righteous, no not one, to make
intercession and stand in the gap for the offenders ;
for these, He, whom they had so grievously and
universally wronged and injured, was contented to
be betrayed and given into the hands of wicked
men.

O the depth of the riches, both of the wisdom
and knowledge of God, who could thus devise such
a way for the salvation of his creatures ! Herein
is love, and the love of Christ constraineth us to
live no longer to ourselves, but to Him that died
for us and rose again. What shall I render to the
Lord for all his benefits? is the first feeling of the
heart; it is a principle of duty that springs out of
the knowledge of the truth received ; it follows as

the natural consequence of our reception of that truth which shows us " we are not our own, we are bought with a price," the precious blood of Christ, as of a lamb without blemish and without spot. Thus, as the apostle says, in Romans, chap. v., " Being justified by faith," (by the belief of this blessed truth,) " the love of God is shed abroad in our hearts by the Holy Ghost, which is given to us ;" that love which had so long flown from man, now returned as a tenant to its deserted dwelling, to cheer, with its enlivening and gladdening presence, a mansion which had never owned another visiter as its rightful master, though it had borne the yoke of many others, " yielding its members servants to iniquity unto iniquity," " serving divers lusts and pleasures," yet finding no comfort or complete satisfaction in any : for his mind, formed as the loadstone for its one great object of attraction, oscillated tremulously in unrest, when not steadily fixed upon " the bright and morning star" of its affections. (Rev. xxii. 16.)

In the Epistle to the Hebrews is also fully explained to us *the way* in which the law of God *could* be again written on the *heart* of man, and obedience to it, in the only acceptable way and spirit in God's sight, rendered possible ; viz. by the pardon of our sins ; for the sense of sin, as we have seen, effectually precluded communion with God, and confi-

dence in him, as well as rendered the *love* of him
impossible. The first covenant (as we are told in
the eighth chapter) having been found incompetent
for these purposes, as the sacrifice for atonement
under it, never could take away sin. " God had
established *a better*, upon *better promises*," " by the
which we draw near to God," " He being merciful
to our unrighteousness, and remembering our sins
no more ;" and all reason to dread and shun God
being by this means removed, He says this is the
covenant I will make with the house of Israel : after
those days, saith the Lord, I will put my laws into
their minds, and *write them upon their hearts ;* " and
I will be to them a God, and they shall be to me
a people :" in accordance with the prayer of Elijah,
" that this people may know that thou art the
Lord, and that *thou hast turned their hearts back
again."*

And we may read again, in the tenth chapter,
this close connexion of the knowledge of the pardon
of our sins, under the Gospel dispensation, with the
law being *re-written* on *the heart of man*, where,
after the completeness of the new covenant had
been contrasted with the imperfections of the old,
the grand *object*, this more perfect covenant was
again declared to have in view, was, that by it " I
will put *my laws into their hearts*," &c. ; for, says
St. Paul, having therefore, brethren, boldness from the

remission of our sins, (by the atonement of Christ,)
to enter into the holiest by the blood of Jesus, let
us draw near, with a true heart, in full assurance
of faith; having our hearts sprinkled from an evil
conscience, and our bodies washed with pure water;
having not only the outward and visible sign of
cleansing in the washing of the water at baptism,
but feeling *this* signified a much more important
thing, the purification of our minds from sin, our
hearts may return to our Maker, like the dove to
the ark again with the olive branch of peace in its
mouth, saying, " Behold we come unto thee, for
thou art the Lord our God."

Every conscientious mind that has ever faithfully
attempted to do its duty in every circumstance of
life, and towards every relative and social tie, must
have felt the want, at times, of one grand leading
principle of duty, to prove, like a compass in the
soul, to guide it with unerring accuracy in the way
in which it should go, through all the mists of uncertainty and error by which it is surrounded.
This, the single eye to God alone supplies, for " if
thine eye is single, thy whole body shall be full of
light," giving us ever one certain aim, guiding us
ever by one pure motive, which leaves no room for
doubt, and gives no opportunity for wavering, and
which, when followed out fully, must be able to extricate us out of all difficulties: and let us be ever

so perplexed what course to pursue, or let it be
ever so difficult to determine what is wisest and
best to be done, our whole duty lies in seeking for
and looking up to Divine direction and aid; and
when we have thus committed our way to the Lord,
and trusted in him with all our hearts, and have
acted according to the best of our judgment, He
who holds us accountable, indeed, for a pure *motive*
and right intention, but does not make us responsible for the success or failure of our plans, forbids
us to fret under disappointment, or repine under
mistakes, as he would have us to be *without care-
fulness*, He says, *when* we have cast all our care
upon Him who careth for us, and to bear with cheerfulness and patience the errors of a fallible judgment, when it has not effected all we desired, for
our own interest and that of others.

And this doing all to the Lord and not to man,
while it elevates the meanest duty of a menial servant to a level with that of the angels who are
" ministering spirits doing the will of God," it
stamps with contempt the loftiest efforts and most
laborious services of man, destitute of *this* one all-
hallowing principle.   It shows us, too, how, like the
Psalmist, we may set the Lord *alway* before us,
for that, not only in the closet on our knees are we
doing Him service, but that we may hold communion with Him equally, and serve Him as effectually,

when going about our daily duty, and engaged in our
most worldly occupation ; for this makes a Bethel
of every place, and gives us a very present God in
every Bethel.

And there are few hours in the day when we
shall not feel the blessedness of having this one
grand subordinating principle in our breasts, to
keep all lesser ones in check, and all our minor
duties in their proper places. For as we are not
allowed to take our feelings merely as a guide in
any duty, or to let the feelings and opinions of
others be a rule to us higher than this, we are supported in a firm persistence in duty, whenever it is
distasteful and repugnant to our feelings, by this
one strong impulse alone, " It is the Lord's will ;"
and we are guarded from allowing the force of our
affection to one object to make us impinge upon the
province of another to gratify our feelings to them,
or from being led, by the encroaching exaction of
a third, to subtract from the duty due to a fourth,
to satisfy them.   And when we find, as we shall
often find perhaps, that, among opposing claims
and conflicting interests, let us hold the balance
ever so even, and strive to give every one their due
ever so carefully, we shall generally fail to satisfy
all, nay, sometimes to please any ; then comes in
the comfort of a higher court of appeal, to which,
as we have primarily and singly sought to acquit

ourselves, we are well entitled to refer our cause,
when the unreasonableness of man denies us that
tribute of approval our conduct may deserve : as
" if our *heart* condemn us not, then have we *confidence* with God," and can say, with his servant of
old, " Behold my witness is in heaven, and my record is on high ;" and however man may defraud
us of our just meed of credit below, " well done,
good and faithful servant," will more than make
amends from the lips of our own Master, to whom
alone we stand or fall.

And those who act from this one high principle,
and this one pure motive, who possess the single eye
and the undivided heart, which refer ever primarily
to God ; and who ask of Him alone, " Lord, what
wilt *thou* have me to do ?" must, from its inducing
a unity of action, be able to exhibit a consistency
of conduct all others are strangers to, who have
many interests to study, and many minds to con-
sult : " for the double-minded man is unstable in
all his ways," and he who has but one to answer to,
and seeks to please but one, is delivered from that
uncertainty of purpose and vacillation of conduct
those are subject to, who are at the mercy of men's
opinions, and influenced chiefly by the fluctuating
events of this ever-changing world. And we need
not fear this sole appeal to God may render men
negligent of attention to the claims and ties of a

subordinate kind below, for we have just seen the
service of God imperatively demands our attention
to every one of these : and that the very principle
of obedience to *Him* must be carried out into every
one of these minor branches ; and we may be assured
we are pleasing Him best, when we are giving the
most satisfaction in that station to which His good
Providence has called us, " doing all as to the Lord,
not to men," "not with eye-service as men pleasers,
but in singleness of heart, fearing God." For we may
observe, that even when St. Paul speaks of becoming all things to all men, it was that "if by any
means he should win some *to Christ*," not to gain
their approbation or secure their affections for *himself;* for he says, " if I should seek to please men, I
should not be *the servant of Christ.*" If a heart
perfect with God, then, is the criterion of Christian
duty, how earnestly should every one humble
themselves in the dust with diligent self-inquiry
and anxious self-distrust ! And feeling that " the
heart *is* deceitful above all things and desperately
wicked, who can tell it? and that God claims the
search of it, as His sole prerogative, how should
every one cry out, " *Search me*, O Lord, and know
my heart !" and seek to lay bare its inmost recesses
to Him, and bring forth its most secret sins, and
slay them before Him. None can ever deceive Him,
though they *may* impose on all around them : as we

may see by the awful disclosure of hypocrisy in
Jer. xlii. 5, 6, &c. What *could apparently* be more
honest and sincere than the language and conduct
of the Jews, who sent to the prophet, saying, " The
Lord be a true and faithful witness between us, if
we do not even according to all things for the which
the Lord thy God shall send thee to us ; whether it
be good, or whether it be evil, we will obey the voice
of the Lord our God to whom we send thee, that it
may be well with us, when we obey the voice of the
Lord our God." Yet He, unto whom all hearts are
open, and who seeth not as man seeth, replies, " *Ye
dissembled in your hearts* when ye sent unto the
Lord your God ! "

And when this " one salt of our sacrifice, love to
God, is lacking," nothing else can compensate, as we
see by the address to the church at Ephesus, when
he enumerates, and gives a careful catalogue of the
many things well pleasing to Him. He observed
there, but though they had shown works and labour
and patience, and for their divine Master's sake had
laboured and had not fainted, yet he says, " Nevertheless, I have somewhat against thee, because thou
hast left thy *first love.*" And in these days of much
bodily service and extensive exertions at home and
abroad for the souls of others, there is too much
reason to suspect, from appearances, the complaints
of the church in Canticles i. 6 is often too appli-

cable : — " They made me the keeper of the vineyard,
but mine own vineyard have I not kept."

But if *those* even, who are engaged *in the work of
the Lord*, and are devoted to his service, may yet
run the risk of growing cold in their love to Christ,
what must be the risk *they* run, who have " returned
like the sow to its wallowing in the mire ?"—and
after having *known* the way of righteousness, and
felt the power of the world to come, and after having tasted of the good word of grace, have gone
back to the haunts of trifling folly, or of impure dis-
sipation ? Though we, as Protestants, know better
what is our true duty to God, than to take refuge
from the temptations of the world in convents and
monasteries, and unlike the unmanly pusillanimity
of the Papist,

" Who, since 'tis hard to conquer, learns to flee;"

we, on the contrary, feel it to be *our* duty *not* to
desert our post in society below; but to stand to
our arms, and, as good soldiers of Jesus Christ, endure hardness, fighting manfully, under the banner
of the cross, against the world, the flesh, and the
devil; assured that, as our Lord has said, " I pray not
that thou shouldest take them *out* of the world, but
that thou shouldest keep them from the evil." He is
quite able to preserve us when we obey His directions, and " abide in our calling;" yet it is too evident that this liberty of Protestants has become an

occasion of much sin to many who have mistaken
their duty in this respect, and imagine that the
pleasures and amusements of the world are hence
become sanctified things to them, or that they have
been, like the fabled hero of old, dipped in some
solution which has rendered them invulnerable to
its snares, and an occasion of grievous injury to
others, who are led astray to their destruction by
their example. But if any conceive that because
the terms used to express the change we undergo
in regeneration, are so strong that they denote a
total destruction of the old principle of evil, as well
as the grafting in of the new principle of good, and
that the God who has brought us out of darkness
into light, is in faithfulness pledged to preserve us,
let us rush into what temptation, or plunge into
whatsoever of trial we may — sad experience will
soon convince them, if the whole testimony of Scripture history fails to do so, that though we *are* so
dead in point of *law*, as that our sinful nature no
longer remains as a barrier to hinder the Holy
One of Israel approaching us—so dead to the law
of works, as that it no longer holds the rod of terror
over us as a hard taskmaster, saying, " do this and
live, and if ye break it ye shall surely die ;" yet we
are not, *in point of fact*, so dead as to any propensity
to sin, or as to feeling any motions of it in the flesh,
or any remains of it in the mind, as to be delivered

from any danger of ever falling into the snares of sin, or being brought again under the galling yoke of the devil; for our Ninth Article very justly tells us, "This infection of nature *doth remain*, yea, in them that are regenerate:" and from the examples set before us in the Bible, we may see, remains an unextinguished, inextinguishable thing, which, till this mortal shall put on immortality, we shall never be wholly delivered from the sad *influence of*, or placed beyond the reach of the danger of being destroyed by. An enemy in the citadel of our heart, that even the holy tenant of the new-born principle of grace can never expel; "for the carnal mind is enmity against God; for it is not subject to the will of God, neither indeed *can be*." (Rom. viii. 7.) The new man is indeed imbued with a principle of obedience, and with the power to vanquish and keep in check the old man, "which is corrupt according to the deceitful lusts: and sin shall not have dominion over us," when being made free from sin, from its yoke, we become servants to God; for though the tempting and temptable thing remains in us, we are not obliged to yield to it; nay, we are without excuse *if we do*, seeing " he that is in us is stronger than all that be against us." And we *may* ever resist, and *always* may " be more than conquerors through Him that loved us." Still our progress must be by a *struggle*, an arduous *crucifixion* of ourselves, and mortification of the deeds of the body, and putting off the old nature; therefore is it fitly described as a " warfare," " a conflict," "a wrestling," " a race," and St. Paul says we wrestle not against flesh and blood, but the principalities and powers, and against the rulers of the darkness of the world, against spiritual wickedness in high places; for that *the flesh lusteth against the spirit, and the spirit against the flesh, and these are contrary the one to the other ;*"—therefore, any who imagine their having embraced any peculiar doctrines, or undergone any complete revolution in their views and opinions, has so secured their interest in another world, as to allow of their taking out the whole good of this world's pleasure and enjoyments, or who, relying on the strength of the antidote religion presents them with, swallow greedily the poison which its society, pursuits, and interests place before them, may be taught, like the man after God's own heart, there is no height of piety we can attain to, which will place us beyond the risk of being, by our own unguardedness and presumption, hurled from thence into the lowest depths of disgrace and degradation; and any who mistake the temporary deadness and disinclination to the world's pleasures, which often ensues under the *first* strong impressions of religion, for a proof that they are now beyond the reach of its seductive

influence; and who, relying upon this present
distaste, enter needlessly into the world, according
to the erroneous proverb too often used, that,
" what is their cross will never be their snare,'
will learn to their cost, that the world can *never* be
so changed in *its* qualities to them, or they so
altered by any change they undergo, as to make it
a safe experiment for the lambs of Christ's fold to
play with the wolves which surround it; for however Satan may vary his mode of attack through
it, and bait his trap with the giddy follies of life for
the young, intellectual for some, and sensual charms
for others, or with the snare of affection and friendship for a few; the principles of the two parties
remain so distinctly different, as to be like heat and
cold, incapable of coalescing, except by the conversion of the one into the other; as " what communion hath light with darkness? and what part
hath he that believeth with an infidel?" And as
the stronger ever conquers the weaker, they must
be fool-hardy and self-confident indeed who reckon
upon subduing the world *to them*, in place of dread-
ing that the world may vanquish them ; for the taste
grows with what it feeds on, and however averse
people may feel to its follies on entering into it, a
relish is as insensibly acquired as a deadness to
higher things imperceptibly creeps over the mind ;

therefore, " let him that thinketh he standeth, take heed lest he fall."

One of the most alarming signs of the times, is the readiness with which men have removed those land-marks which the piety and wisdom of their ancestors erected between the church and the world, and have entered not only into a parley but a compromise with the enemy. So that now no line of demarcation remains to point out to the young Christian, wherein lies the difference in pleasures, studies, and occupations, between the two parties; and the most distressing symptom to every pious mind of the deadly nature of the disease in the christian body, and the hopelessness of the case, is, that the Lord withholds his chastisements, and "Ephraim is joined to idols, *let him alone*," seems the awful sentence gone forth against such transgressors. God seems to be "giving them up to a strong delusion to *believe* in a lie;" he feedeth on ashes, a deceived heart hath turned him aside, so that he cannot deliver his soul, or say, Is there not a lie in my right hand?" For when our Lord bids us pray *daily* not to be led into temptation, if he see us voluntarily rush into it, which *He* even could not do, refusing to tempt the Lord his God, as Satan wished Him to do, to put the extent of His preserving mercy to the test in casting himself down from the pinnacle of the temple, because God had said he should give his angels charge over him lest at any time he dash his feet against a stone; —we can hardly expect Him to work a miracle for our rescue, when we refuse to use the *means* placed within our power for our preservation.

If the former generation erred in laying too great a stress on outward separation from the world, and, by exalting unimportant peculiarities, and descending into trivial and minute particulars, laid a stumbling-block needlessly in the way of weaker brethren, and in stretching the line too tight broke it altogether often, surely the present generation have gone into a very unnecessary extreme in the opposite direction. It is said "extremes meet;" and the reverse of wrong, so far from being necessarily right, may, from the powerful force of reaction, carry a person into a yet greater error than that from which they have escaped; and if the one party erred, therefore, in going so entirely out of the world as to forsake their relative duties, are the others then obliged to run entirely *into* all its scenes of vanity to perform theirs? Surely not! No one commandment of God requires to be fulfilled by disobeying another; and it must be the result of utter ignorance only, that can make us suppose that, to enable us to obey God, we must leave our duty to our fellow men undone, or in

doing our duty in that station of life to which God
hath called us, we must inevitably neglect our duty
to the Great Giver of all commandments. If the
generation, then, who preceded us, thought that,
provided they erected a screen between them and
the world to secure outward separation from it,
it mattered little what unholy tempers and dispositions, covetous practices, and dishonest dealings
were exhibited behind it, shall we who confess that
we know *better* than this, by our censures of them,
and have learned wisdom by their fault, rest excused if we not only cut off the heads of the weeds
as they did, but see that we tear up also root and
branch of the evil? And if they, in renouncing
the world, found it a much more difficult task to renounce themselves, even with all the advantages
which separation from the world and leisure
afforded them; shall we, who add temptation to
difficulty, and unguardedness to temptation, find it
an easier one, without all these helps to aid us, and
with all these obstacles to hinder us, to do so?

And if we give not God this proof of our sincerity
in doing directly "that which is least," and lies
within our power, can we expect his assistance to
enable us to do " that which is most," and *beyond*
our power, as truly self-conquest is? Would it
not be a safer and a wiser course, to resolve that *our*
conduct shall be more consistent, shall combine *all*

the requisites we *know* to be called for, when we are
aware that nothing short of the complete conse-
cration " of our *whole* body, and soul, and spirit,"
can be deemed satisfactory by God? and, while
others erroneously thought cutting off merely the
right hand of fellowship with the world was enough,
to determine to pluck out the right eye which is
evil within also, and to be careful to cultivate whatsoever things are true, whatsoever things are
honest, whatsoever things are just, whatsoever
things are pure, whatsoever things are lovely and of
good report, than to catch a mere peculiarity of
phraseology and preciseness in external things?
If it be affirmed, as it often is, that we see less of
dissensions in families, fewer irritable tempers, and
less of alienation and uneasiness among friends in
consequence of conformity to the world being admitted of, we grant it, as the great cause of dispute is removed, the great bone of contention is
given up, the parties are now assimilated, the church
has become a part of the world, and the world has
no occasion to quarrel with her allies and patrons;
the conversation, aims, and pursuits all harmonize,
so that there is no ground for dispute and dislike. There is great peace in a country when
a conqueror has subdued it, and enslaved its inhabitants. But is this a desirable peace? There is

a great calm and stillness with a dead corpse, but
is this an enviable calm ?

Too many pens, nay too many pulpits, now-a-days,
vindicate this system, and people are rejoicing too
much in the modern discovery that it *is* possible
to serve God and mammon, to render this a welcome
statement; and "this is a hard saying, who can
hear it?" most minds will answer. Yet as higher
authority than any man's, however high that man
may be that advances it; nay, higher than that of
all men, has decided differently, the writer feels it
to be a duty to warn every man, and testify to every
man, that thus saith the Lord, "Whoso is a friend
of the world, is the enemy of God, " and " whoso
loveth the world, the *love of the Father* is not *in
him.*"   And surely these days of unwonted peril,
and notorious delusions, are not the ones to try so
hazardous an experiment. Nay, in place of this,
they call loudly and solemnly on all to add an hun-
dredfold of watchfulness, vigilance, earnestness,
and self-distrust, to their conduct, beyond all that
went before ; and though they are not only permitted, but commanded, to remain at their post of
duty, even though their lot may be cast " where
Satan's seat is," they are to do it in a spirit of
dependence upon Him, who has promised to keep
them from falling, and to present them faultless

before his throne. And in the use of all those means for their defence He has provided them with, " taking to them the whole armour of God, that they may be able to stand against the wiles of the devil, having their loins girt about with truth, and having on the breastplate of righteousness, and their feet shod with the preparation of the Gospel of peace ; above all, taking the shield of faith, and for an helmet the hope of salvation and the sword of the Spirit, which is the word of God, praying always, with all prayer and supplication in the Spirit, and watching thereunto with all perseverance, " harmless and blameless as the sons of God, without rebuke, in the midst of a crooked and perverse generation, among whom they shine as lights in the world." Though *in* the " world" in no one sense of the world, but crucifying the flesh with its affections and lusts, which all incline to and hanker incessantly after it, they die daily to it, "for whatsoever is born of God overcometh the world, and this is the victory that overcometh the world, even our faith, by which the world is crucified to us, and we to the world ;" we, looking to all its pomps and vanities as a dying man hanging on the cross would view them, who felt *he* had no longer any interest in them, but must set his hopes and desires on other and better things, pass through this life in a spirit of habitual self-denial, as those who are "no

longer debtors to the flesh to live after the flesh,"
which has only brought us sin, and sorrow, and
death, but sowing to the Spirit, which "has begotten us" again to a lively hope, by the resurrection of Christ from the dead, to an inheritance incorruptible, undefiled, and that fadeth not away,
reserved in heaven for us. In place of sitting down
as those who *can feel*, or wish to *find* contentment
and satisfaction in the things of this dying world,
we, as true servants of our divine Master, who had
not where to lay his head, pass on our way as
strangers and pilgrims, abstaining from fleshly lusts
which war against the soul, and taking up our
cross, follow him, "declaring plainly that we seek
a country, a better country, that is an heavenly,"
"choosing rather to suffer affliction with the
people of God, than to enjoy the pleasures of sin
for a season."

Of all offensive states for men's minds to be in,
the one God seems to regard with the greatest
abhorrence, is a state of indecision and indifference,
or, as it is styled by Him, "lukewarmness." "Thou
art neither cold nor hot; I would thou *wert* cold or
hot." (Rev. iii. 15.) Absolute coldness, or deadness, were a less revolting spectacle for God to
witness, it appears, than that of a person knowing
and acknowledging Him to be the only satisfying
portion of the soul, and his service as its proper

duty, and who yet has not sufficient resolution to yield up himself wholly to Him, or devote himself heartily to His service; yet is it not evident, that this is the state of the majority of professing Christians at this moment? many owning it by their free confession, and many more by their conduct; unmoved by the awful threatening of our Lord, " So, then, because thou art lukewarm, and neither cold nor hot, I will spue thee out of my mouth" as a thing too loathsome to be tolerated by Him who *so loved us*, as to die for us; and "*greater* love hath no man than *this*, that a man lay down his life for his friends:" and if *we* can afford *Him* only half our hearts in return, and a very small portion of our time and thoughts, we shall find, as David warned his son, " that the Lord searcheth the hearts and understandeth all the imaginations of the thoughts, and that if we seek him He will be found of us, but if we forsake Him he will cast us off for ever," and assign us no portion with *his saints*, " who counted not *their lives dear to them*," and " counted the loss of everything but as dung and dross, that they might win Christ and be found in Him; nay, were tortured, not accepting deliverance, that they might attain a better resurrection."

Let none rely upon numbers as constituting safety, and think, because so many thousands are

in the same state, it is impossible *all* can be wrong,
which is often the sole reason for many embracing
or persisting in a system, and which, so far from
being in favour of the truth, is, according to Scripture, one of the strongest proofs to the contrary ;
for we are told, true spiritual believers will always
be in the minority, and a little flock in this dispensation ; for strait is the gate and narrow is the
way to eternal life, and *few there be* that find it,
so that *number* is a weight generally in the wrong
scale below; and the very thing to increase our
suspicion that all is not right.

But there is a sin connected with this subject,
against which a heavier woe yet is denounced,
" *Cursed* is the man that trusteth in man, and maketh flesh his arm, and *whose heart departeth from the
Lord ;* for he shall be like the heath in the desert, and
shall not see when good cometh, but shall inhabit the
parched places in the wilderness, in a salt land and
not inhabited." (Jer. xvii. 5, 6.)   Now, though the
way in which the temptation to this sin most easily
besets us, probably is in the ensnaring influence
which the ties of relationship or affection exert over
us, stealing our hearts from God, yet the terms employed point to a degree of dependence, and an
extent of confidence reposed in the creature, which
God demands as due to Him only, and no mere mortal should presume to claim ; and perhaps there

is no commoner nor more insidious form under which *this snare* presents itself to us, than in the idolatrous devotedness with which men now-a-days regard their favourite preacher. But so little are the objects of this temptation aware of the sin of thus supplanting their Divine Master in the affections of His flock, that it is coveted as the commendable aim of their exertions; and so little are their deluded followers alive to the danger *they* run in thus allowing their Creator to be eclipsed by the creature, that though many a star has fallen from heaven of late, as if crying aloud in their ears, " Cease ye from man ;" yet though all join heartily in this cry, when one of these idols *falls* from the place of dangerous exaltation they had elevated them to, yet it is forgotten when they are *rearing up another*, for then it is reiterated with unabated vehemence, " The man is everything." And to such a length has this evil extended, not only among dissenters, but in the northern church of our land, that *personal preference* for the individual is acknowledged as the sole ground for the deferential respect and reverence of a congregation towards their pastor; and in place of an individual claiming respect primarily *by virtue of his divine office*, that holy office is alone respected, and his person tolerated, when he can bring the human gift of eloquence to its aid ; and consequently God's house, " which was to be a *house* of prayer for all nations," is now oftener transformed into a theatre for the display of fine oratory.

But we would rather turn from this melancholy picture, to contemplate the beautiful *contrast* the prophet holds up to our view in the seventh verse : " Blessed is the man that trusteth *in the Lord*, and whose hope the Lord is : for he shall be like a tree planted by the water, and that spreadeth out her roots by the river, and shall not see when heat cometh, but her leaf shall be green, and shall not be careful in the year of drought, neither shall cease from yielding fruit."

Let this then be our earnest prayer, that both the writer and the reader may, from their own blessed experience, be enabled to say with Ephraim, as quoted by the prophet Hosea, chap. xiv. ver. 8, " What have *I* any more to do with idols ? I have heard Him, and observed Him—I am like a green fir-tree : from me is thy fruit found ! " " For I will be as the dew unto Israel, saith the Lord ; he shall *grow* as the lily, and cast forth *his roots* as Lebanon," (the outward growth is described as small, compared to the deep *inward* growth of the Christian.) " His branches shall spread, and his beauties shall be as the olive tree, and his smell as Lebanon.

Many who are sensible of the danger of *worldly* associates, and alive to the guilt of compliances

with worldly customs, and take warning by the fate
of Jehoshaphat, whom the seer went out to expos-
tulate with, saying, " Shouldest thou help the ungodly, and *love them that hate the Lord? therefore is
wrath upon thee* from before the Lord,"—are yet too
too apt to imagine, that if they are among religious
people, or with pious friends, they are in no danger of having their heart withdrawn from God : but,
alas ! there is so much worshipping of the creature,
building up one another in self-conceit, and so much
mutual self-delusion at present existing in religious
circles, from the prevailing unfaithfulness to each
other, and keen sensitiveness to reproof or censure,
that leads to a cloking and hiding of each other's
sins, in place of an honest testifying against them —
and, in fact, any one who attempts such a thing, is at
once cast off by all—that there is as great danger
there as anywhere else ; nay, fully greater, from
our being, perhaps, more off our guard ; and we
may soon find, that not without a very significant
meaning has St. John placed at the end of his first
Epistle to believers his last and most solemn of all
warnings, " Little children, keep yourselves from
idols." For we are also too apt to imagine, that if
the ties which bind us to our fellow-men are only
sanctified by religion, there can no harm arise to us
from indulging to excess in them, but the holiest
human being may, by standing between us and our

Maker, intercept the light of His countenance from us as effectually as a more unworthy object : and if they engender a sense of dependence on them, so as to become to us the rod and the staff on which we lean in this vale of tears ; or if they accept of that homage of an appeal to their judgment and reference to their opinion as a definitive settlement of all questions, and solution of all difficulties; or if, under the influence of their authority or presence, we are assiduous in many duties which we utterly neglect when away from them, our heart is not whole *with God*, our eye is not heaven-directed. We are no nearer to God than we were before ; we are "men-pleasers" only, and have done all to man, and not to God ; and as the spring can rise no higher than its source, our reformation will be wholly of that superficial, external kind, that is "eye-service" only, and we can gain no higher reward than that approval of men, which we alone aimed at in all we did ; and whatever advances we may make in virtue, or even piety, we shall have to begin all over again, and must act from a *new* and wholly different principle, when we commence our "walk with God !"

The position the church of Christ is to assume in the last days, we are told, in the eleventh of Revelation, is that of "witnesses." The seven churches we see are dwindled away to two, (fourth

verse,) and these are described as in the attitude of
witnessing, more as isolated individuals than as
large compact bodies; and this, combined with other
descriptions of the situation of the church in the
latter days, leads us to infer, that perhaps scattered
individuals, "few and far between," existing in the
professing churches, or almost choked with the
worldly tares which surround them, will constitute
those mystical members of Christ's body, which His
day is *not* to overtake as a thief in the night, as it
will the ungodly, but whom it will find " children of
the light and of the day," " with their loins girded
about, and their lights burning," waiting and ready
for their Lord's return, prepared to enter in with
Him to the marriage supper.   And though we may
not have yet fully arrived at this exact position, or
reached this critical period, we are fast approximat-
ing to it; and, as witnesses, are called upon now, to
lift up the voice of our testimony against the abound-
ing of iniquity, and overspreading of abomination
all round us.

    A *silent witness* is a contradiction in terms ; for
whilst the world's idea of amiableness and goodness
is a smiling with equal complacency on all the good
and all the evil around us ; and never to wound the
feelings of any, by the affronting suspicion, or alle-
gation, that we think they are doing what they
ought not to do ; the christian witness dares not thus

countenance wickedness, or confound virtue with
vice, as to make no distinction in his manner towards
it: nor thus stain his conscience with blood-guiltiness,
by refraining to testify against all the evil he sees
around him. Yet *should* any be even placed in that
subordinate situation in which silence *is* an impera-
tive duty, or in that painful one, when to speak
were but to cast pearls before swine, who would
turn again and rend him"—still, nothing can exonerate him from bearing a faithful witness against sin,
by his conduct, in carefully avoiding all collusion
with it, participation in it, or sympathy towards it,
and in steadily persisting in an opposite course of
holiness and virtue; and this silent perseverance in
right, and abstinence from wrong, has often more
weight, and often proves a severer rebuke to those
who do evil, than any words..

Let not the young Christian who attempts thus
ever to stem the torrent of sin and folly he en-
counters, expect that he will meet with any reward,
or any assistance here below, from those around
him, and that the eye of satisfaction will beam on
him, or the voice of approval strengthen his heart
at the trying moment, and second his efforts to
escape a snare, or persist in a duty; for there is
something in the human mind, even of those we
might expect better things of, that makes men
shrink with dislike from any attempts at superiority,

singularity, or unsociableness; and the dogged resistance, or shrinking back of the tender conscience,
may meet with no word or look of encouragement
from the bystanders, whilst the yielding of the
overcome scruples of the weak is, perhaps, hailed
with a shout of triumph, or an air of pleasure, by
all around; for there is something apparently en-
gaging and amiable (especially on the part of the
young) in a complying spirit, or a deferential con-
ceding to the wishes and opinions of others; whilst
the reverse wears the aspect, perhaps, of self-opi-
niativeness, or obstinacy; therefore, he who seeks
to do his duty faithfully to his God, must be con-
tent, in the mean time, with the testimony of his
own good conscience alone, and must wait patiently
for his reward from God, at his day of future judgment. But how few are there who *can* thus re-
linquish all present reward, and wait patiently for
this distant prospect of recompense for their "work
of faith, and patience of hope, and labour of love?"
And fewer still are those who can encounter the
sneer of contempt, the eye of scorn, and, above all,
the overwhelming torrents of *ridicule* it invariably
calls down upon them; worse to bear than all the
rest put together. We need not wonder, then, that
the witnesses are spoken of as consisting of two
only—

" Faithful found among the faithless."

For our Lord warned us that when " iniquity should
thus abound, *the love of many* would wax cold."
It is impossible to open our Bibles without being
struck with the prominency there given (in descriptions of men's character, prospects, and fate)
to the state of *the heart;* by it, we may see, God
forms his estimate of men, and it is ever taken as
an index to their spiritual condition. A " heart
perfect with God" is described as the right and
healthy state of the soul; " a heart not whde"
with him, as a most unsatisfactory state to be in ;
" a heart alienated from God" by wicked works, or
" departed from him," as the most miserable and
wretched state of any ; and " a heart at enmity with
God," as the highest degree of guilt, and most
dreadful state of rebellion.

It is stated to be the cause of all, too, that is
amiss in men's conduct, as their sin is traced up to
a fault *there* as to its fountain head ; " for as yet
the people had not prepared their hearts unto the
God of their fathers ;" and " he did evil because he
prepared not his heart to seek the Lord ;" and is
given, too, as the reason of their advance in all that
is good, that " the people *had* prepared their hearts
to seek the God of their fathers ;" and had " entered into a covenant to seek the Lord God of their
fathers with all their heart, and with all their sous;
and ye shall find me, when ye shall seek me with

all your soul, and I will be found of you, saith the Lord; and I will cause him to draw near me, for who is he that engaged his heart to approach unto me, saith the Lord?" " For the eyes of the Lord run to and fro through the earth, to show himself strong in behalf of those whose heart is perfect towards Him."

But whilst the thought of this is full of comfort and peace to the sincere believer, who, in reply to the question of his Lord, " Lovest thou me?" can lay his hand upon his heart and say, " Lord, thou knowest all things, thou knowest that I love thee, even whilst owning with deep self-abasement, in the words of a saint of the last century—

" O loved—but not enough—though dearer far,
Than life and its most loved enjoyments are,"

and who may take comfort from the gracious words in Isa. lvii. 15—" For thus saith the high and lofty one that inhabiteth eternity, whose name is holy : I dwell in the high and holy place; with him *also* that is of a contrite and humble spirit, to revive the spirit of the humble, and to revive the heart of the contrite ones ;" it is one fitted to fill the undecided, and far more the hypocrite, with anxiety and terror, " whose hearts God knoweth, for he only knoweth the hearts of the children of men," and who can be deceived by no mere lip service, or mere professions, however ardent, " for hell

and destruction are before the Lord, much more
the hearts of the children of men ;" and who tears
aside every veil which sophistry or insincerity may
wrap around itself : " for this people draweth near
to me with their lips, but have removed their *hearts*
far from me, and their fear for me is taught by the
precept of men ;" and " though with *their mouth*
they show much love, yet *their heart* goeth after
covetousness." Who that reflects upon this can re-
frain from exclaiming, " Who can understand his
errors ? O cleanse thou me from my secret sins !"
And who is there but must feel the force of the
wise man's advice—" Keep *thy heart* with all diligence, for out of it are the issues of life ?"

CHAPTER VII.

AND whilst we see how the knowledge of the forgiveness of our sins, through the blood of Christ, enables us to obey the first table of the law, we come now to see how it prepares us for obeying the second, " which is like unto it, Thou shalt love thy neighbour as thyself," for this is the love of God, that we keep his commandments ; " and this is my commandment," saith our Lord, " that ye love one another, as I have loved you ;" " for the end of the commandment is charity, out of a pure heart, and of a good conscience, and of faith unfeigned ;" the pure heart, we have seen, is the heart purified by *faith*, for no heart is pure by nature ; and the good conscience, St. Peter says, " we have, through baptism ; not the putting away of the filth of the

flesh, but the answer of a good conscience towards
God." (1 Pet. iii. 21.)

Thus, whilst a sense of forgiveness restores us
to our Maker, it reconstructs also, and replaces on
our hearts, that most excellent gift of charity, the
very bond of peace and of all virtue, without which,
whoso liveth is counted as dead before God, which
connects us in the bonds of peace with our fellow
men. The one duty flows, indeed, naturally out of
the other, as St. John shows us, " Beloved, if God
so loved us, we ought also to love one another, for
he that loveth him that begat, loveth him also that
is begotten of him;" and " he that loveth not, *knoweth
not God*, for God is love ;" and " if we have not the
Spirit of Christ, we are none of his," for love is of
God, and he that loveth is born of God, and knoweth
God ; in this the children of God *are manifest*, for
He that has begotten us expects to see the image
of the Father reflected in the children ;" as obedient
children, not fashioning ourselves according to our
former lusts in our ignorance, when we are described as " hateful, and hating one another," but
testifying that He who is love is in us, " because
He hath given us of *his* Spirit ; " for if we love one
another, God dwelleth in us, and His love is perfected in us.

The new commandment that our Lord, under the
Gospel, gave His disciples, was, that " they should

love one another, that by this *one* distinguishing
feature in their character," all men might know
that they were His disciples in that they had *love*
one for another, which remains a command as binding upon *us* at this day, as it was on *them* at its
first promulgation, and a mark that ought to be as
observable a one of distinction to point us out to
the notice of every one, as it unquestionably did
them; but, alas! on the contrary, may more now
be taken as a rule by which we can prove most professing Christians to have none of that faith
which worketh by love, than as a means by
which we can infallibly discover them from the
world around them! Yet are we told, on no other
ground can our love to God be accepted, except
inasmuch as it has wrought in our breasts the same
feelings of kindness, mercifulness, forbearance, and
forgiving dispositions, we have ourselves met with
at the hands of our heavenly Father; for, "if a man
say I love God, and hateth his brother, he is a liar,"
says the Scripture; "for if he love not his brother
whom he *hath seen*, how can he love God whom he
hath not seen?" and this commandment have we
from Him, that he who loveth God love his brother
also.

And can this be deemed an unreasonable re-
quirement? that if the blessing of him who was

ready to perish, rises from our lips in our secret
chamber to God, who has plucked us as brands
from the burning of eternal ruin, and remembering
our affliction and misery, the wormwood and the
gall of our former lost condition, our soul hath them
in remembrance, and is humbled within use; we
yet come forth thence, in the spirit of strife and
debate, with every angry temper and proud feeling
within us unaltered, to smite with the fist of wickedness, or with the yet more cruel and deadly scourge
of the tongue, " to cause our voice to be heard on
high." " Surely He that is higher than the highest
regardeth ;" and if thou afflict them in any wise,
and they cry unto me, 1 will surely hear them, for
I am merciful, saith the Lord, and my wrath shall
wax hot ;" and " the Lord God of recompense shall
surely requite," for the cries of the oppressed shall
come up as a memorial before him, to cancel all
our supplications for pardon and for grace ; " for
with what measure ye mete, it shall be measured
unto you again ;" and " he shall have judgment
without mercy, that showed no mercy."

It is also given unto us as a sure text by which we
may try ourselves, whether Christ Jesus is in us,
or whether we be reprobates. For " *hereby* we are
to know that we *have passed* from death unto life,
because we love the brethren ;" and whether also we

have passed from darkness unto light, for he that
saith he is in the light, and hateth his brother, is
in darkness even until now : he walketh in darkness, and knoweth not whither he goeth, because
that darkness hath blinded his eyes ; which shall
be opened too late by the light of eternity, showing
him his portion must for ever be in those regions
of darkness where the light of hope never shines
again ; nay, upon our faithful performance of this
duty of loving others as God hath loved us, we are
told hangs a yet more important consequence to
us, even our own acceptance at the last day ; as
our Lord has bid us recall daily to our memory, in
that prayer he framed for us, expressly he says,
to teach us that " if we forgive not men their trespasses, neither will our Father which is in heaven
forgive us our trespasses."

And unpalatable as this truth must be to many
ears, still none can disannul the word of God, however they may dislike or despise it ; and most as-
suredly, whether we believe it or not, " the word
which I have spoken," says our Lord, " the same
shall judge them in the last day;" therefore it
would be a wiser course to prepare ourselves *for*
that judgment by rendering ourselves fitted for its
searching trial, than by shrinking from the thought
now, or neglecting to do so, feel the full weight of
its awful effects, when it is too late to avoid them.

We may see this fact strikingly illustrated, that if we use not the mercy now given to us, as *a motive* and as *a means* of showing mercy to others in this day of grace, the mercy we have enjoyed, so far from being of any avail to us in the day of judgment, will only heighten our offence, and serve to aggravate our guilt; in the parable of the two debtors, (Matt. xviii.,) which, even had we no other passage of Scripture more explicitly declaring it, would, of itself, be sufficient to convince us *a judgment according to works* is to succeed to a *justification by faith.*

Our Lord had been giving his disciples some directions upon the subject of forgiveness of injuries, which led to Peter inquiring how *often* it would be expected *of us* to pardon those who offended us, should we be called upon to do it, were the offence against us even seven times committed, when our Lord replied, " I say not unto thee until seven times, but until seventy times seven;" evidently implying by this, that as there was no bounds to *God's forgiving* mercies to *us*, there could be none in *ours* towards our fellow men: therefore He says is the " kingdom of heaven likened unto a certain king, which would take account of his servants; and when he had begun to reckon, one was brought unto him which owed him ten thousand talents; but forasmuch as he had nothing to pay, his lord commanded him to be sold, and his wife and children, and all that he had, and payment to be made. The servant, therefore, fell down, and worshipped him, saying, Lord, have patience with me, and I will pay thee all. Then was the Lord of that servant moved with compassion, and loosed him, and forgave him the debt. But the same servant went out, and found one of his fellow servants which owed him an hundred pence; and he laid hands on him, and took him by the throat, saying, Pay me that thou owest;" but the mercy he had himself so lately experienced had not, it seems, melted his heart into a feeling of compassion and sympathy for similar woes, for it remained, as appears by the story, hard still as the nether mill-stone; nor did he even feel bound by any sense of honour and justice to copy the glorious example his own Master had just showed him, to whose goodness it was owing that he stood there, a free man, possessed of all he held dear on earth, with an opportunity of exercising the same blessed privilege of doing to another as he had been done by; but in the spirit of unrelenting cruelty, though " his fellow servant fell at his feet, and besought him, saying, have patience with me, and I will pay thee all," he would not, but went and cast him " into prison till he should pay the debt.''

But though the blush of shame, and the pang of

remorse did not tinge his own cheek, and visit his
own bosom, his conduct did not pass unnoticed
even below ; and we may do well to remark here,
that however little the world ever deem the commands of God binding on *themselves*, they consider
His servants as imperatively called upon to obey
them; nay, are acutely sensitive as to the very
smallest deflexion they may make from the path
of duty, which, whilst it will form one of the
most awful testimonies against *unbelievers* at the
last day, proving they were by no means *ignorant*
of what God required from man, should form also
an additional reason for Christians looking well to
their ways, and avoiding even the *appearance* of
evil, lest they cause the name of God to be blasphemed among men through their misconduct ; for
people are well entitled to expect to see us walking unblamably and unreprovably before all, and to
expose us if we do not.

But to return to our history.   " So when his
fellow servants saw what was done, they were very
sorry, and came and told their Lord all that was
done : then his Lord, after that he had called him,
said unto him, O thou wicked servant, I forgave
thee all that debt, because thou desiredst me;
shouldest not thou also have had compassion on
thy fellow servant, even as I had pity on thee ? And
his Lord was wroth, and delivered him to the tor-

mentors," till he should pay all that was due unto
him. And lest his disciples should not have made
the faithful application of it that was intended, our
Lord brings it home to the case of every individual
believer, by saying, " So likewise shall my heavenly
Father do also unto you, if ye, from your hearts,
forgive not every one his brother their trespasses ;"
showing us clearly that *there will be a future judgment* upon the pardoned and justified believer ; and
showing us, too, what *the principle* of that judgment
will be, viz. a trial of us to see whether the mercy
we have received at our Maker's hands, has
wrought in our hearts " all mercy and all good
fruits," " forbearing one another, and forgiving one
another, if any man have a quarrel against any,
even as God for Christ's sake hath forgiven us."

This awakening and startling truth, that our restoration to the favour of God, through forgiveness, has
been merely the introducing us into a probationary
state, to enable us to acquire suitable tempers and
dispositions that shall qualify us to be the children
of " the God of our mercy," and partakers of his
kingdom, receives much light, by a careful comparison of the Epistles of St. Paul and St. James, who,
in severally treating of these two different points of
doctrine, " justification by faith" and "justification
by works," as they both term it, have chosen the
same person to illustrate their separate views, and

o 2

not, we may believe, without a very deep and significant meaning, as it is evidently intended to show
us, these two different events take place in each individual's experience, and often at very different
periods of their life.

In the fourth chapter of Romans, we see how
strongly and pointedly St. Paul insists upon it, that
Abraham was justified *by faith alone* without the
deeds of the law; for he justly observes, " For if
Abraham had been justified by *works,* he *had* whereof
to glory; for to him that worketh is the reward
not reckoned of *grace,* but of *debt ;* but to him that
worketh not, but believeth on Him that justifieth
the ungodly, his faith is counted for righteousness."
And it is impossible to read the 3d, 4th, 5th, and
6th chapters with a candid mind, open to conviction,
and anxious to understand what the Scriptures
really mean, and not to *give* its statements the meaning we wish, or had designed beforehand they
should give, and not allow that St. Paul makes out,
beyond a doubt, " that a man is justified by faith,
without the deeds of the law," for " by the deeds
of the law shall no flesh be justified in God's sight."

If we turn then to St. James, we shall find that
there is no *real* discrepancy in the two statements
which have perplexed many minds ; but that, like the
introduction into music of an apparent discord, it
only more exquisitely elicits the harmony of the

whole piece; for we shall find, that when St. James
affirms so confidently that Abraham was justified
by works also, *he* is adverting to *another event* at a
much later period of Abraham's life, which, far from
overturning St. Paul's statement, all the more
strongly confirms it; and that whilst St. Paul had
been treating of Abraham's entrance into the church
of God, by faith, St. James is speaking of an after
period, when that faith had budded and blossomed,
and brought forth fruit unto holiness, by his having
been put to the test of trial, and when, having been
weighed in the balance, he was *not* found wanting :
and therefore, argues the apostle, " was not our
father Abraham justified by works, (subsequently
we see,) when he had offered Isaac his son upon
the altar. We see, then, how faith wrought with
his works, and by works was his faith made perfect; and the scripture was *fulfilled*, which saith,
Abraham believed God, and it was imputed unto
him for righteousness, and he was called the friend
of God : ye see, then, how that by works a man is
justified, and not by faith only." In fact, it needed
this *proof* of works to testify to its being a true
faith : yet it stands to reason he must have been
primarily justified by faith, to have enabled him to
bring forth the fruits of faith, or to bring forth the
fruits of the Spirit, which holy Spirit we only " receive *through* the hearing of faith." Therefore, as

there must ever be a cause to produce an effect, we must be sure this relates to the justification of a believer, not to that of a *sinner*, as our tenth Article plainly tells us, " The condition of man after the fall of Adam is such, that he *cannot* turn and prepare himself by his own natural strength and good works to faith, and calling upon God, wherefore we have *no power* to do good works, pleasant and acceptable to God, without the grace of God by Christ preventing us, that we may have a good will, and working with us when we have that good will." And to this justification by works, or final judgment of a believer, so many of our Lord's parables refer, such as that of the talents, the sheep and the goats, the ten virgins, &c. which all refer to a season of present privileges conferred on us in this day of grace, to be succeeded by a trial of our use or abuse of them at a day of judgment.

The other instance of justification by works which St. James cites, is strongly confirmatory of this view, for we may, by referring to Rahab's history, perceive *she was a believer*, ere she did those works by which St. James tells us she was justified ; and such a triumphant confession of faith, in her review of God's past works and prophetic anticipation of the future as she made, (Joshua ii.,) is unexampled in such circumstances as hers perhaps, and seldom equalled under tenfold *her* advantages ! Though generally some space of time elapses for the proof and trial of our faith, ere we reach the goal of victory, yet there has been one instance recorded, where the conversion and the crowning of a sinner were almost simultaneous : and the thief on the cross, who made confession unto salvation to his Saviour, was assured by His lips that " that day should he be with Him in paradise ;" but, as has been often, and never can be too often remarked, " there *is one* instance, that none should despair ; and *but one* instance, that none should presume." Too many, however, take the exception for the rule, and strengthen the bands of wickedness in the *living*, by the false comfort they indulge in when speaking of the *dead*, and by the way in which they buoy up the minds of departing sinners with false hope ; and too many, again, allow of no exceptions at all to the rule, and so quench the smoking flax in despair, which a little sound scripture encouragement might have fanned into a flame.

But to resume our description of *what* this principle is, of "faith, which worketh *by love*," and by which love, exhibited in our daily life and walk, all men are to ascertain, and we ourselves are to prove ourselves that we are Christ's disciples, we come next to observe, that it is not a love that is to evaporate in mere empty expressions of kindness and of friendship, but we are told must disclose itself in active beneficence, and deeds of mercy, like the love of Him "who went about doing good;" for "true religion and undefiled before God and the Father is this," says St. James, "to visit the fatherless and widows in their affliction, and to keep himself un-spotted from the world;" (James i.;) for if a brother or sister be naked and destitute of daily food, and one of you say to him, Depart, be ye warmed and filled, notwithstanding ye *give* not those things which are needful for the body, what doth it profit? (chap. iii. 15, 16,) And St. John is equally explicit on the subject, who says, "Whoso hath this world's goods, and seeth his brother have need, and shutteth up his bowels of compassion from him, how dwell-eth the love of *God* in him?"—the love of *Him* on whom the eyes of all wait for food, and He giveth them their meat in due season. If *our* love, then, be empty-handed cold and hard-hearted, it bears no re-semblance to *His*, who filleth all things living with plenteousness, and who appoints the rich their por-tion, merely to give them the privilege of being the stewards of His bounty below to the *poor*, and the happiness of knowing that " it is more blessed to give than to receive."

The wide, active, comprehensive range this cha-rity is to have, our Lord shows in Matthew xxv., wherein he tells us, not only are the hungry to be fed, and the naked to be clothed, but the stranger is to be sheltered, the poor visited, the sick relieved, as if every sufferer we met with in human flesh were our *Lord himself,* who suffered for our sins ; as he tells us he shall take every such mark of attention as a personal mark of regard to Him, and every proof of neglect as a personal insult done to himself, for inasmuch as ye did it, or did it not, "to one of the least of these my brethren, ye did it, or did it not, unto *Me.*" But, whilst we are thus warned, the mere feeling, unaccompanied by the action, amounts to nothing in God's sight ; we are equally taught that the mere action, unless it is prompted by the right spirit, and springs from the right motive, is equally unacceptable to Him ; " for though I give all my goods to feed the poor, and have not charity," says St. Paul, " It profiteth me nothing." Not the most self-denying sacrifices, the most energetic exertions at home, and the most extensive missionary enterprises abroad, can compensate to God for a heart destitute of this grace, which should be the very pivot on which all these turn ; and not all the posthumous endowments of our splendid bequests *at death,* for establishments for the good of the bodies and souls of men, can ever atone to God for the absence of this feeling in our hearts during *our lives.* Nor must we hope that the disbursement of all our worldly goods will ever lay up for us treasures in heaven, if we do so " to be seen of men ;" for our

Lord bids us not let our left hand know what our right hand doeth, that our alms may be in secret, and our Father, which seeth in secret, may reward us openly. If we seek man's approbation, verily we *may* have our reward below ; our names may be engraven on monumental marble, to carry down the fame of our good deeds to many generations, or it may be engraven on the yet more pleasing tablets of the grateful human heart ; when the ear heareth us, it may bless us—when the eye sees us, it may glisten with thankful joy, so that we may taste, in its most exquisite sense, the luxury of doing good, yet may we have no reward of our Father which is in heaven, who, so far from allowing us to covet this lesser fruit of our labours of love on earth, forbids us, " whose praise is not of men but of God," to accept of it ; for says He, " How can ye believe which receive honour one of another, and seek not the honour which cometh of God only, following His example, who says, " I receive not honour of *men*," for " the reward of the righteous shall be given them."

And this brotherly love, wherewith we are taught of God to love one another, must be no love of flattery or of favouritism, as it is equally to be without partiality as without hypocrisy ; and in place of its allowing us to blind ourselves to the sin of the object of our fondest affections, or tempting us to hide their defects from our sight, we are bound by the sacred tie which unites us, to be *faithful* as well as *affectionate*, and " to exhort one another daily, lest any of us be hardened through the deceitfulness of sin :" which was a duty as plainly enjoined under the law as under the gospel. " Thou shalt not hate thy brother in thine heart—thou shalt in anywise rebuke thy neighbour, and shalt not suffer sin upon him," (Levit. xix. 17,) regarding our neglecting to warn a person in danger *of losing* their soul by remaining in their sins, as tantamount to *hatred!* And under the Gospel we are not only forbid to have any fellowship with the unfruitful works of darkness, but we are desired to *reprove* them, (Eph. v. 11,) as it would be better, had we the christian courage and magnanimity so to do, to run the risk of losing the favour of a friend here, than to let him run the risk of losing his soul eternally, through our timidity, time-serving, or self-seeking.

But it is to be done in the spirit of meekness, considering ourselves lest we also be tempted, obeying the golden rule, " As ye would that men should do unto you, do ye so even unto them." A deep consciousness of our sin, weakness, and infirmities, instilling tenderness, consideration, and kindness into all our remonstrances, will prevent our wounding the feelings unnecessarily, or stirring up the feelings of resentment it will excite in most bosoms, more than is possible. And whilst we are bound to bear

a true witness against the *sin*, even of those we love
most dearly, we must as carefully beware how we
allow the sin and imperfection we see and suffer
from in others, ever to alienate our attachment from
them, or wear out our patience with them; for we
must " endure the contradiction of sinners against
ourselves," as our Lord did, "who pleased not himself," and as our heavenly Father does, "who is
kind to the unthankful and to the evil;" for "if we
love them only that love us, what thank have we?
and if we do good to them that do good to us, do
not even the publicans the same?" And unless
our righteousness under the Gospel shall exceed
the righteousness of the scribes and pharisees under
the law, we shall in no case enter into the kingdom
of heaven.

The spurious kind of love that now passes current
in the world for the true, nay, not only in the world,
but is too common among professors of religion, is
little more than a mere cheating ourselves into the
belief of the existence of all those amiable qualities
which we see no evidence of in the conduct, or in
the persuading ourselves that there is an absence of
all those evil dispositions which we see too many
proofs of the existence of in the temper and conduct of those around us; a mere " calling evil good,
and good evil—a putting of bitter for sweet, and sweet
for bitter," so unworthy those whose " love is to be

without dissimulation," that, " for the truth's sake which dwelleth in us," should be for ever banished from christian communities, who are privileged and enabled to love on so much higher and purer grounds, that they are not obliged to resort to any such miserable fictions to perform their duty.

" One who can love us while he reads us true,"—(KEBLE,) sets us an example of a much holier and higher species of love, as well, as we have seen, by granting to us His own Holy Spirit to dwell in us, confers on us *the power to be like Him* in this, and every other particular in which finite minds *can* imitate the Infinite. His is a love of no sympathy in the sin, though of tender compassion for the person of the sinner ; of no winking at the transgression, but looking it steadily in the face with every feeling of abhorrence ; is a holy, disapproving love, which was shown in His sending his Son to bless us *in* turning away every one from his iniquities. Therefore, as we are permitted and commanded to love all around us from this strong principle of duty, let us not put on the mere semblance of the feeling from lower motives, " for Christ our Passover is sacrificed for us ; therefore let us keep the feast, not with the old leaven, neither with the leaven of malice and wickedness, but with the unleavened bread of *sincerity* and *truth.*" The world is indeed obliged to resort to this mere fiction and imitation of the heaven-born principle, because it has *no better* and no higher ground to go upon, and as it is the only bond which holds society together, we need not quarrel with it, but we may respect it, though we are not called upon to copy it; and as they can conceive of no love but that which arises from reciprocity of affection, or which is founded upon real or fancied esteem, the love which animates the Christian's breast is either regarded as an enigma beyond their powers of solution, or denounced as hypocrisy or insincerity. For if there is no ground in their opinion for affection; or if they are deceived, and find the object of their attachment does not possess those qualities which command respect or attract love ; or if they do anything to forfeit it, they consider themselves justified in withdrawing their affections, and all men will regard them as doing no more than what is right in casting them off for ever. But the Christian lies under a solemn obligation *to love* on, in spite of all, and through all ; as, seeing *his love* is not founded on the qualities to obtain it the person possesses, and not owing to man for his *own* sake, but for the sake of his Saviour, so no misconduct of man can absolve us from the debt we owe him, no want of estimable disposition can cancel *that* bond ; therefore is the command one of perpetual obligation, to " owe no man anything, but to love one another." For let a man deserve anything, however harsh or severe, at our hands for his *own* sake, we are, for the sake of Christ, to love our enemies, do good to them that hate us, and pray for them that despitefully use us and persecute us.   For it is the will of God, that as we cannot render *Him* any service " who is far above our sight," that we should show our gratitude to *Him* by our kindness to all the creatures of His hands below.   And let us be ever so deceived in the objects of our charity, or ever so uncertain of the genuineness of their wants and woes, we may console ourselves with the reflection, " he that receiveth a righteous person in the name of a righteous person shall receive a righteous person's reward ;" as the sin of the deception will be visited on the deceiver, not on the deceived. The love of the worldly is little else than a sympathy in sin, or a mere system of concession, as the old proverb says, " let alone for let alone ;" or, you wink at my sin, and I will do the same to you.   And by the sort of *charitable* excuses (as it is termed) people make for the sins of *others*, we may judge how they could wish and expect *their own* offences to be palliated and extenuated by society.   But most contrary is this to true Christianity ; our love to the person of the sinner, we must again repeat, should be joined to the strongest feeling of disapproval of their sins, and the most honest and ingenuous testimony against them.   And hence arises the discord often observable in families from the introduction of true

religion among them; and hence are accounted for the
two opposite statements of the effects that it was
to produce, that our feet which are to be " shod
with the preparation of the Gospel of peace," yet will
often prove the means of " setting a man at vari-
ance against his father, and the daughter against
her mother, for a man's foes shall be those of his
own household." Persons may live in peace and
quietness all their days, let them hold what peculiar
opinions they may, or practise what personal aus-
terities, or indulge in what eccentricities they like,
as long as they leave others undisturbed; but the moment they attempt to show others there is no rule
binding on them which does not equally affect them
also, and no truths they hold which do not equally
belong to them—in a moment they arouse every angry
feeling of the human heart, and their very name is
cast out as evil for their dear Master's sake : for as
all human friendship and affection is founded on mutual good opinion, or this compact of a mutual
compromise regarding imperfection, the moment a
person admonishes any around them they are not
walking according to godliness, they think they have
fallen in their esteem, and consequently have forfeited their regard; and hence spring alienation of
affection, resentments, and recriminations, and all
those fruits of that enmity to the cross of Christ,
which is not ceased, and never *shall* cease in this
dispensation, which often is a great cause of per-

plexity, of stumbling and alarm to the weak disciple
who has never sufficiently attended to or perhaps
forgotten his Lord's word, " Suppose ye that I am
come to send peace upon earth ? I came not to send
peace, but a sword." But in place of sinking into
despondency or trembling with apprehension, " he
should rejoice and be exceeding glad, for so perse-
cuted they the prophets which were before them."
To those Christians to whom all this is an unknown
trial, or "an hard saying, who can bear it?" we
would reply, Woe unto you, when all men speak
well of you, says your Lord, it is no *good* sign ;
you are without *one* proof that you are *His* children
who says, " If it hated me it will also hate you ; it
hated me before it hated you," and you possess a
proof few would *wish* to possess, that you are one of
the world, "for the world will love its own ;" the world
cannot hate you, as our Lord says, " but *me* it hateth,
because I testify that the works thereof are evil."
But woe also to those who exhibit an equally war-
like aspect with their foes; and it is very difficult, as
the eloquent writer of Felix Neff observes, to carry
love in the heart unquenched when the sword must
be ever in the hand : yet if we render "evil for evil, and
railing for railing," and are overcome of evil, in place
of overcoming evil with good, we are not bearing a
true witness as " the children of our Father which
is in heaven, who maketh his sun to shine upon the

P

evil and the good, and sendeth rain upon the just
and the unjust." And if any think it hard to bear
even *this small* portion of suffering, which now-a-
days falls to the believer's lot below, what would
they have done in those days, when men were led
to prison and to death for their Redeemer's sake,
and suffered the loss of *all things,* and the disrup-
tion of the nearest and dearest ties; yet " took
joyfully the spoiling of their goods, knowing in
themselves they had a better and more enduring
inheritance?" If thou hast run with the footmen and
they have wearied thee, how canst thou contend with
the horses ? and if in the land of peace wherein thou
trusted they wearied thee, how wilt thou contend
with the swellings of Jordan ?

It is hard, it is a *very* painful trial, to see the eye
of affection that once beamed on us, averted, the
warm feelings of cordial intercourse chilled and in-
terrupted, and all this, by the very thing that, were
men's minds as they *ought* to be, would be a reason for
increased affection and esteem: but would it not be
worse, even allowing this trial its fullest weight, and
admitting its greatest degree of suffering, to have
Him whom we have pierced with our sins, and
wounded with our iniquities, at the great day when
we shall behold Him eye to eye in the midst of as-
sembled worlds and angels, cast the same look of
reproachful anguish upon us as He did when He

turned and looked upon Peter, who went out and wept bitterly? *He* had space given him for repentance below, but to us, then, repentance will be unavailing; for our Lord tells us, "Whosoever shall be ashamed of me and of my words in this generation, of him shall the Son of Man be ashamed when He shall come in his glory with the holy angels."

Once more, this love is to be extended, we are told, not only to the bodies but to the *souls* of our fellow creatures, as our Lord instructs the penitent Peter, on restoring him to His favour and forgiveness, showing him, he could best exhibit the sincerity of his love to his merciful and gracious Master, by feeding the lambs and the sheep of His flock. And if the rewards are great to those who attend to the wants of the perishing bodies of men, how much greater are those which are promised to such as take care of the wants of their never-dying souls! "They that turn many to righteousness, shall shine as the stars for ever and ever." (Dan. xii.) Nay, "he which converteth *one* sinner from the evil of his way, shall save a soul from death, and shall hide a multitude of sins." (James v. 20.)

But as this duty is better understood than many others in the present day, and is well illustrated by many abler pens, the writer may be excused enlarging upon it, as the object of this little work is rather to explain duties of a less obvious nature,

and those which at present are perhaps more over-
looked. We may understand, even from this slight
sketch of the christian duty, why it is said, " love is
the fulfilling of the law," for we may see that this
one principle encloses in itself all others, like the
one pure ray of light (to reverse the simile) which,
when passing through the prism, is broken down
into the several beautiful hues of which all colours
are composed ; so this one principle of love is capable of universal application, and can adapt itself to
every relation and circumstance of life, addressing
itself with equal facility to each : for when in operation it must make a man a good father, a good
husband, a good son, a good brother, and a good
master of a family, as well as would ensure his being a loyal subject ; for viewing the powers that be as
ordained of God, "whose he is, and whom he
serves," he knows he is doing his God service in
being subject to *them*, and " fear God and honour
the king" are inseparably bound together in his
mind ; it also equally insures his being a sound
patriot, as he is a promoter of that righteousness
which exalteth a nation.   In fact, under the influence of this principle, when it was in full operation
in any man's mind, no crime could be committed,
and no duty could be left undone, for love worketh
no ill to his neighbour ; therefore would the hand of
the oppressor be removed, the dishonest would cease

to defraud his neighbour, and the voice of the slan-
derer and the blasphemer would be no longer heard
in the land. And as "the sun would never go down
upon our wrath," but all anger and clamour, and
malice and evil-speaking, would be removed or re-
pressed, the peace of a neighbourhood would be but
little disturbed, and the long deep resentments that
perpetuate enmity would endanger no man's soul
by their indulgence, and bitter words break the bond
of friendship in twain no more. And ambition and
the lust of power being quenched in men's breasts,
by "each esteeming others better than themselves,"
men would beat their swords ere long into plough-
shares, and learn war no more. Did they allow this
principle full sway over their minds, the very
beast of the field would taste its blessed effects, as
" the merciful man is merciful to his beast." But
besides this negative operation of doing no harm to
our neighbour, this principle lays us under the positive obligation of doing to the utmost all the good
that is in our power: and as this obligation exists
in the debt we owe to *God*, and not from any that
man can claim at our hands, it is one of universal
extent, as well as of perpetual continuance, as the
necessity for paying it can end only with our lives,
or with the absence of every object for its exercise:
so that till no sick-bed remained to be soothed, no
prisoner sighed through his grated windows for re-

lief, no mendicant ever lifted a supplicating eye, and no voice of anguish met our ear, or was within the reach of our hand or means, there should be no pause in our efforts, there could be no excuse for the termination of our labours.

If it be objected, there is no such principle in existence, because we see so little of its effects in operation, we deny the right of any to judge of a law merely by the obedience paid to it, as we must examine what the law says itself, not measure its exactions by men's compliance with its demands. And the unbelief of man cannot make the faithfulness of God of none effect," that " if men had walked in His ways, and kept His testimonies, He should soon have put down his enemies ;" for " O that thou *hadst* hearkened unto my commandments " is his affecting reproach to us, " *then* had thy peace been as a river, and thy righteousness as the sands of the sea." Nor shall man's unbelief, nor his perversity, blessed be God, make the faith of God of none effect in the realization of those grand events, and glorious promises, which refer to a higher and holier dispensation than that under which we live: when he assures us, " righteousness *shall cover* the earth," at length, " as the waters cover the depths of the sea," for my people *shall be all righteous*, and they shall inherit the land for ever; the branch of my planting, that I may be glorified." However men may *now* defeat their Lord's gracious intentions and desires, and Satan may, for a time, frustrate them, the hour is coming, " when as the garden causeth the things that are sown in it to spring forth, so the Lord God will cause righteousness and praise to spring forth before all the nations:" when the accuser of the brethren shall be cast down, and bound with a great chain, and " the whole earth is at rest, and is quiet, and they break forth into singing, How art thou fallen from heaven, O Lucifer, son of the morning !" The very *few* specimens we are permitted to see, in this our day, of the effects of this holy principle, when in full operation on the heart and conduct, which makes it to us like "meeting as it were an angel unawares," falling in with them, may enable us to form some idea, however faint, of the day—*now* we trust not *afar* off, but a day *nigh* at hand when " holiness unto the Lord" shall stamp *all* the vessels of the Lord's house, and the way shall be the way of holiness, along which the unclean can never pass.

But we must also recollect, the unbelief of men can never make the faithfulness of God of none effect, in that "the day cometh," too, " that shall burn as an oven, when the proud, yea, and *all* that do wickedly, shall be as stubble, and the day that cometh shall burn them up, saith the Lord of Hosts, that it shall leave them neither root nor branch." Yea, and

that we are to connect this threat, under the *Law,*
(Mal. iv. 1,) with that of our Lord under the *Gospel,* that it is " *a fire* that *never* shall be quenched;"
" for if they escaped not who refused Him that
spoke on earth, how much more shall not *we* escape
if we refuse Him that speaketh from heaven ? For
God, who at sundry times, and in divers places, spake
unto our fathers by the prophets, hath in these last
days spoken unto us by His Son, and *how shall we
escape if we neglect so great salvation !*" Men's merely
disbelieving a future judgment will not deliver them
from it, or absolve them from falling under the effect of it, but their *believing* it here, and living
under the influence of it; and " herein, like the
apostle, exercising themselves to have a conscience
void of offence towards God and towards man," will
effectually deliver them from its fatal effects ; for if
we have known and believed the love of God in de-
livering us from the present evil world; and if
this love of God to us, says the apostle, has filled
us with love to God and all men, then, " he that
thus dwelleth in love, dwelleth in God, and God in
him; and *herein* is our love made perfect, *that we
may have boldness at the day of judgment,*" because,
" as He is, so are we in this world." *Christ,* for His
own merits, enjoyed the favour of God, as a perpetual sunshine on his soul : and *we for His sake* only,
never for our own merits, are joint heirs with Him in

the favour of God now.   And if we now are " the
sons of God, when he shall appear we shall be like
Him, for we shall see Him as He is."   When He
who is our life shall appear, *then* shall we also appear
with Him in glory," whose lives have been hid with
Him in grace; for *then* shall the righteous shine forth
as the sun in the kingdom of His Father. " I ascend
unt o *my Father* and *your Father*," saith our Lord; " and
if I go and prepare a place for you, I will come again,
and receive you unto myself, that where I am, there
ye may be also ;" and we shall be heirs *with Him* of
a kingdom that fadeth not away, reserved in heaven
for us who are kept, by the power of God, through
faith, unto salvation.

   To conclude, " Happy is the man," saith St.
Augustine, " who loveth his friend in thee, and his
enemy for thy sake." And " as many as walk according to *this* rule, peace be on them ! " " for the
fruit of righteousness is sown in peace, of them that
make peace."

CHAPTER VIII.

THIS, then, is that christian confidence, which
" makes none ashamed that trust in it;" and one
well worthy of the name, being founded on no false
view of God's character, and on no fiction concerning our own ; on no false hope that God may prove
to be less holy in His nature, and less righteous in
His judgments with us, than we imagined ; or that
we may prove less guilty, and so have less reason
to dread encountering that final judgment, than
our faithful monitor, Conscience, had represented.
But a confidence, founded on a real knowledge of the
truth of God's awful majesty, and our own great un-
worthiness, and which yet allows of our " fleeing
for succour to Him, who for our sins is justly dis-
pleased ;" and of our " committing our souls into
His hands, *in well doing*, " as to a faithful Creator,"

" who is able 'to keep that which we have committed to Him against the great day." A confidence, worthy of being given by " a God of Truth
and uprightness," to creatures made in *His* image ;
and who, however they may have degenerated from
their high original, yet retain such an instinctive
sense of what is needful for the peace of their minds,
as to be unable to rest satisfied on any less secure
basis ;—a confidence so sufficient for our present
comfort, as to " keep them in *perfect peace* whose
minds are stayed on it," and to fit them for all
duties, and to fortify them for all difficulties ; for
" in quietness and in *confidence* shall be your
strength ;" as well as to still all anxious misgivings
with respect to their prospects of finally attaining
the mark of their high calling ; they " being con-
fident of this very thing, that He who has begun
the good work in them will continue and perfect it
against the day of the Lord Jesus," " for what He
hath *promised* He is able also to perform ;" and one,
too, which enables him to look the last and worst
enemy of his soul, Death, in the face without
alarm ; for " the peace of God, which passeth all
understanding, shall keep his heart and mind in
the knowledge and love of God, and of his Son,
Jesus Christ our Lord." A confidence which no
calamity can deprive him of ; yea, though he should
lose the whole world, and everything, and every one

in it he holds dear; for as it is one " the world
cannot *give*," so is it one " the world can never
take away" by any of its reverses or bereavements;
and it is one, also, which no disease of the sin-sick
soul can ever defeat the efficacy of, save that which
consists in a careless neglect, or obstinate rejection
of the means of cure; for our Lord has said, " All
manner of sin and of wickedness shall be forgiven
unto the sons of men, and blasphemies wherewith-
soever men have blasphemed, but blasphemy against
the Holy Ghost (a scornful contempt, or sinful distrust of His power to save) shall never be forgiven,
neither in this world, neither in that which is to
come." A confidence which does not spring from
our selfish and indolent natures being relieved from
the burden of duty, but from a delightful assurance
of ability being given us to enable us to fulfil it;
for " I can do all things through Christ strength-
ening me," is its language; nor yet from the necessity of conquering sin being removed, but from
a sense of power to overcome it being granted to
us, " for the weapons of *our* warfare are not carnal,
but mighty through God to the pulling down of
strongholds, casting down imaginations, and every
high thing that exalteth itself against the knowledge of God, and bringing every thought into cap-
tivity to the obedience of Christ."

Nor yet does it consist in our being set at liberty

to revel in the delights of the flesh, and so takes from us all fear of the consequences of indulgence in the pleasures of this dying world; but in its imparting to us a counteracting principle, strong enough in our soul to supplant all these lesser enjoyments in our affections, (or conquer their power over our minds,) and able so to fill and satisfy the desire of our minds, as to deprive us of all our restless cravings after inferior sources of comfort; " for he that drinketh of the water that I shall give him," says our Lord, " shall never thirst ; but the water that I shall give him shall be in him a well of water springing up into everlasting life."

Nor is ours a confidence like the Arminians in ourselves, in the assurance that our own efforts, if faithfully and perseveringly used, will be quite sufficient to obtain our salvation, binding us thus, like the galley slave, to the oar of duty all our days, for the purpose of procuring the favour and forgiveness of God, through our own deserts; but as it is a confidence which rests on a salvation already accomplished for us, " by Him *who hath saved us*, and called us with an holy calling, not according to our works, but according to His purpose and grace, *which was given to us in Christ Jesus*, before the world began," forbids of our entering upon our duties from any such purely selfish motive, but

allows of our commencing them in a happier frame,
and from the holier and higher principle of " fulfilling all the good pleasure of His goodness, and
the work of faith with power." For we, being now
assured that the favour and forgiveness of God *was
procured for us* by Christ; and that the perennial
showers of His goodness are descending upon our
souls *for His sake*, " who when we were without
strength died for us," being now strengthened by
His mighty Spirit in the inner man, we are strong
in the Lord, and in the power of *His might;*
and being strengthened thus with all might, according to His glorious power, unto all patience,
and long-suffering with joyfulness," we " go on our
way rejoicing," from strength to strength, " walking and praising God," as the lame man did whom
Peter restored to the use of his limbs at the beautiful gate of the temple ; "*for the joy of the Lord is
our strength*," " and in his name do we rejoice all
the day long."

" Leaving, therefore, the principles of the doctrine of Christ," as the apostle recommends, (Heb.
vi. 1,) " we go on unto perfection; not laying
again the foundation of repentance from dead works,
and of faith towards God; of the doctrine of bap-
tisms, and of laying on of hands," &c.; for this
foundation being once laid, when we become believers, we, like wise master-builders, proceed to

rear hereupon the superstructure of a holy life; and " building up ourselves in our most holy faith, praying in the Holy Ghost," " we all, as lively stones, are built up, a spiritual house, an holy priesthood, to offer up spiritual sacrifices acceptable to God by Jesus Christ," and not as if we had already attained, either were *already perfect;* but this one thing we do, forgetting those things which are behind, and reaching forth to those things which are before, we press toward the mark for the prize of the high calling of God in Jesus Christ;" for we do desire that every " one of you do show the same diligence, to the full assurance of hope to the end," says the apostle, (Heb. vi.;) and so says St. Peter, " Wherefore, also, the rather, brethren, give diligence to make your calling and election sure, for if ye do these things ye shall never fall: for so an entrance shall be ministered unto you abundantly into the everlasting kingdom of our Lord Jesus Christ."

Thus we see, that though the assurance of faith, viz. a knowledge of God's gracious feelings and intentions towards us, hails us at our entrance into the divine life, proclaiming *to us all,* that " to us is born a Saviour, Christ the Lord;" and that through His name whosoever believeth in Him shall receive remission of their sins; yet that the full assurance of hope, though it appears in the distance as the prize to be attained, yet is never reached fully till faith is lost in sight, and hope in full enjoyment: "for hope that is seen is not hope, for what a man seeth, why doth he yet hope for? but if we hope for that we see not, then do we with patience wait for it." (Rom. viii. 24, 25.)   The one is, as it were, the first step of " the ladder set upon the earth," which we put our foot upon in believing ; the other is that which rests on heaven, which we only finally reach when " mortality is swallowed up in life."

Yet, though hope thus springs out of obedience, duty, as St. John shows us, also springs out of hope ; they produce thus, and reproduce each other, for " he that hath *this hope in him* purifieth himself, even as he is pure." Well, then, may St. Peter say, " Blessed be the God and Father of our Lord Jesus Christ, which, according to His abundant mercy, hath begotten us again to *a lively hope* through the resurrection of Jesus Christ from the dead," which, as we have shown, is intimately connected with *our* being raised from the death of sin to the new birth of righteousness, " which hope we have (who have flown for refuge to the hope set before us in the Gospel) as an anchor of the soul sure and stedfast, and which entereth into that within the soul," as the apostle shows. (Heb. vi. 19.)

If any wish for a surer ground of confidence than this, such an one as sets a mark upon them at the outset of their earthly career, insuring them of their final safety, and informing them, to a positive certainty, of the result of its final close ; this, the assurance of salvation, they may, indeed, we grant, find in many of man's systems of divinity, but we cannot find for them in God's word, wherein we see comfort and peace of mind so identified with, and so inseparably bound up with, holy obedience, that any severance the apostle compares to the dissolution of the tie which holds body and soul together, (James ii. 26,) and, consequently, any confidence which can exist apart from this, the only unquestionable evidence of its existence, must be, as our Lord describes the state of those " whose works He had not found perfect before God," " having a *name* to live when *we are dead.*"

Such a confidence, the apostle, who had been in the third heavens even, did not possess, for *he* tells us, " *I* keep under my body and bring it into subjection, lest that by any means, when I have preached to others, I myself should be a cast-away." Such a confidence, distinct from, and irrespective of, our faithfulness and obedience, our Divine Teacher and Master was unacquainted with. " Not every one," He says, " that *saith* to me, Lord, Lord, shall enter into the kingdom of heaven ; but

he that *doeth the will* of my Father which is in
heaven; *many* will say to me in that day," (by
this we may see how extensively the error shall prevail,) " Lord, Lord, have we not prophesied in thy
name, and in thy name cast out devils, and in thy
name done many wonderful works?   And then will
I profess unto them, *I never knew you—*depart from
me, all *that work* iniquity.   Therefore, whosoever
heareth these sayings of mine, *and doeth them,* I
will liken him to a wise man, which built his house
upon a rock; and the rain descended and the floods
came, and the winds blew and beat upon that house;
and it fell not, for it was founded upon a rock. And
every one that heareth these sayings of mine, and
doeth them not, shall be likened unto a foolish man,
which built his house upon the sand, and the rain
descended and the floods came, and the winds blew
and beat upon that house, and it fell, and great was
the fall of it." (Matt. vi. 24—27.)

Here we see, that though *Christ* is even called
the Rock of our salvation, yet we can only have *a
part* and lot *in that rock,* can only be fixed there
and made *one with Him,* by having his indwelling
Spirit within us, " making us fruitful in every good
work;" for if we have faith without works, this is
no more than the devils have, " for the devils *believe* and tremble;" and " every branch in me that
beareth not fruit," says our Lord, " He taketh away;

and every branch that *abideth* not in me is withered, and men gather them and cast them into the fire, and they are burned :" therefore does He say, " Be thou faithful unto death, and I will give thee the crown of life."

If any imagine we shall hence be tempted, like the legalists, to say, when we have, *through the Spirit,* made any advances in holiness, " By the strength of *my hand* I have done this, and by *my wisdom,* for I am prudent," " sacrificing thus to our *own* net, and burning incense to our *own* drag," as Habbakuk describes it, we, knowing that " it is *God who worketh in us,* both *to will* and *to do* of His good pleasure," and that " *we are made perfect by his comeliness which he puts upon us,*" (Ezek. xvi. 14,) shall be as little able, as we probably shall be inclined, to boast ourselves of our riches, as was the poor prodigal disposed to be of " the best robe" his father put upon him, and of the ring on his hand, and shoes on his feet, which were *the gifts* of his father's gratuitous bounty, not the fruits of his own deservings. And so far from any attainments of ours ever allowing of our instituting a claim of merit upon God, and exacting heaven as the reward of our works—our Lord tells us, " when we have *done all*, we are unprofitable servants ; we have done that which it was our duty to do," for *we owed God*

a debt of implicit obedience, and we do but pay
Him that which we owe Him when we keep His
commandments, and are no more entitled to demand compensation at His hands, for so doing, than
is the dumb animal entitled to do at ours, who dies
in its harness, after having expended the flower of
its health and of its strength in our service. And
though we have " respect unto the recompense of
reward," it is because we know " it is the Father's
good pleasure to give us the kingdom" " which He
hath promised to all them that obey him ; and because our Lord hath told us, " we shall be recom-
pensed, at the resurrection of the just," with, " Well
done, good and faithful servant, enter thou into the
joy of thy Lord ;" for " to him that overcometh will
I grant to sit with me on my throne, even as I also
overcame, and am set down with my Father on his
throne."

But some are apt to mistake, because St. John
has, in consequence, said, " He that doeth righteousness is righteous, for every one that doeth
righteousness is born of Him;" that we may hence
infer the positive safety of a man, if we only see
him do the thing that is right, however ignorant
we may be of the principles from which his good
works proceed ; for that, provided God finds much
fruit on a tree, when he comes to examine it, he will

be satisfied, without caring of *what nature* that fruit may be. But though it is undoubtedly the fact, that no good tree can ever be barren, but must testify to its healthy root by its loaded boughs, yet many a fruitful tree below, pleasant to the eye of man, may bear only " grapes of gall and bitter clusters," lovely to the sight, but utterly distasteful to Him who seeth not as *man* seeth, but who trieth the very reins and the heart; for we have plainly shown from Scripture, that those good works *only*, which spring from a right motive, and are directed to a right end, can find acceptance in *God's* sight, or have any reward of our Father which is in heaven; and the righteousness St. John speaks of is not mere virtue and good works, in the *world's* acceptation of the term, but such a one as He can own and bless.

There are now many falsehoods and fictions abroad, on the score of *charity;* and because our Lord has said, " judge not, that ye be not judged," people think themselves absolved from His command, " judge not according to appearance, *but judge righteous judgment;*" and that the more dishonesty of mind they practise, provided it is on the side of leniency to sin, and kindness to wickedness, the more pleasing it will be to Him, who is *the truth*, as if He, whose name and nature is essentially such, should impose upon his children the necessity of

constantly violating *it*, to fulfil that most important
duty of charity, " without which all our doings are
as nothing worth" in his sight ! Consequently,
many who are under this impression, imagine that it
is right to believe that he who says, " thou shalt
not make to thyself any graven image, thou shalt
not bow down to them nor worship them," and who
says, that " at the name of Jesus every knee shall
bow," can yet be as well satisfied with the worship
of the papists and the pagans, addressed to images
of wood and stone, that their own fingers have made,
and with that of the Mahometans and the Socinians,
who refuse to allow his Son that divine nature which
constitutes his title to be worshipped, as he is with
the worship of true believers ; forgetting that it is
said, " He that justifies the wicked, and he that con-
demneth the just, *even they both* are an abomination
to the Lord."

But, however men may deceive themselves in
this day with such fancies of their own imaginations,
the hour is at hand which will tear the veil of delusion from their eyes, by exhibiting God's just principles of judgment before all, and " *then* shall they
return and *discern* between the righteous and the
wicked, between him *that serveth God* and him *that
serveth Him not.*" In the same spirit is the idea
which prevails, that because St. Paul has told us, in
the second chapter of Romans, " That the Gentiles

which had not the law, yet who did by nature the
things contained in the law, these not having the
law, but being a law to themselves, &c., shall be
judged without the law, and by that law of nature
written on their hearts, and faithfully obeyed, that
therefore those, at the present day, living under the
noontide blaze of Gospel light, who yet prefer to
walk by the faint glimmer which the light of their
own conscience affords them, in place of taking the
higher authority of revelation as their guide, shall
be judged according to this lesser light they have
chosen, and shall escape the severe judgment of
God's written word given us in the Gospel; but such
as affirm this may do well to recall to mind, that St.
Paul expressly tells us " the time of this ignorance
God winked at, but *now commands every man every-
where* to repent;" for " the darkness *is past*, and the
true light *now shineth*," says St. John, and they who
voluntarily turn their back upon the sun, shining
in its strength, and love the darkness better than
the light, and " who stumble and fall, and are
broken," like the blind at mid-day, have every
chance of " being reserved in the chains of darkness against the judgment of the great day." Can
any suppose, that had Cornelius, the Gentile soldier,
who feared God with all his house, and gave much
alms to the people, and prayed to God always, when
God, in answer to his prayer, vouchsafed him yet

purer light, and bid him send for Peter, who should tell
him words, whereby he and all his house should be
saved, rejected God's proffered mercy, and preferred
walking by the partial light he possessed, affirming it
was quite sufficient for his salvation; that his prayers
and his alms would *still* have "come up as a sweet
memorial before God," when he thus presumed to
dictate his own terms to the Almighty, by which
he chose to be saved, and refused to accede to those
of God's own appointment? We cannot suppose it,
any more than we can deem any safe who throw
themselves thus on a mere *chance* for salvation, and
reject the *certain* mode of attaining it God has
placed within every man's reach in the Gospel.

Those who object to the doctrine of a confidence,
founded on a knowledge of a present pardon, as being contained in the atonement, may be reminded
here, that every objection which they bring against
it, for fear of the consequences which *they allege*
must follow in its train, applies with equal force to
that forgiveness which our Lord granted to different
persons when on earth; and yet the fear of such
fatal results to the morals of men, as now men prog-
nosticate must occur, never hindered Him saying,
to any poor, penitent believer, "Thy sins are forgiven
thee, go in peace." Nor do we ever hear of such
effects following the announcement, as indeed it was
very unlikely they should do, when the whole tone

and tenor of His instructions taught such a different lesson ; and when " go and sin no more," and " sin no more, lest a worse thing happen unto thee," taught the recipient of the blessing the use he was expected to make of it.

Nor did it, probably, ever occur to our church, when her children return to her at confirmation, to be admitted, by their own act, into her bosom, where they had been placed, as unconscious infants, by their sponsors at baptism, that when she lays her hands on their heads, and tells them, " There is given unto them the forgiveness of all their sins," referring to their baptismal ablution, of which this is the ratification, that they would infer from this, they were forthwith relieved from the necessity of ever seeking for pardon from any sin again, upon a repetition of transgression; as, on the contrary, she teaches them every sabbath that they enter her courts, that though they ought *at all times* humbly to acknowledge their sins before God, yet ought they most chiefly so to do publicly; when they assemble and meet together ; and puts into their mouths a confession every way fitted to bring the sins of every human being to their remembrance, and of so humbling and heart-searching a nature, as to apply to every case.

Though such a well-grounded confidence in God as this is which we have been describing, is at all

times needful and desirable for our soul to enable us
to draw nigh to God, and to put that trust in Him
which constitutes our own peace and safety, and to
offer Him that praise which glorifies Him; yet,
surely, there never was a time in which such a
shelter for the soul seemed so imperatively called
for as at the present moment; for whether we listen
to such as have studied prophecy, and who account
for the present convulsions which rend society by
telling us we are fallen upon those evil days when
the last and most dreadful vial of God's wrath was
to " be poured into the *air*," which was to produce
thunders, and lightnings, and a great earthquake in
the intellectual region—which was to be the arena
on which the last awful conflict between the church
and her enemies was to be enacted; or to the fore-
bodings of men of mere worldly wisdom, one * of
whom, a few years ago, remarking upon the dis-
cordant elements he observed coming into play in
men's minds, said, " he foresaw a worse war at
hand than any that had hitherto devastated the world,
—a war of opinions." And another of whom,† who
belongs to the party that have precipitated these
judgments upon us, published his warning to his
party, in a few pithy sentences in a leading journal
of the day lately, telling them, that owing to their
rapid strides in revolutionising the country, there

* Mr. Canning.   † Rev. S. Smith.

were "but a few years more left for the church
and the monarchy in this land." We must be con-
vinced, that there is a power at work, seeking to
unsettle men's minds, and to overthrow the existing
order of things, such as, we have before quoted,
"never was from the foundation of the world," and
such as, blessed be God, "never again shall be"—
and which calls upon each of us to be prepared and
fortified for a fierce assault: for " these are but the
beginning of sorrows," which, except they should be
shortened, there shall no flesh be saved : but which,
for the elect's sake, we are told, shall be shortened.

These, then, are not the days to lure us back into
an indolent and superstitious reliance upon the authority of any church, or the advantages of any
peculiar external forms and modes of worship, to
insist on a blind unreasoning submission of the
intellect, or an unintelligent acquiescence in any
dogmas, or any customs, or to attempt to bring about
a uniformity of opinion in peculiar points. As well
might men try to bind the winds in a tempest, as to
do so now, when the spirit of unrestrained freedom
of opinion and license of principle is abroad, and
when any effort to do so only contributes to increase the discord, and widen the breach which now
separates mind from mind below. Now is the moment, on the contrary, to seek to embue every
mind with those grand unalterable primary prin-

ciples of their common faith, which shall stand
them in good stead when all these auxiliary sup-
ports shall vanish from their grasp: for, let us
turn a deaf ear to the voice of alarmists as we may,
whether they speak on the authority of prophetic
announcement, or from the dictates of their common sense alone; still, our own *eyes* must convince
us, that the infidel and liberal spirit of the day has
gone forth on a crusade against every sacred, char-
tered, and prescriptive right in the land : and as
we were forewarned that " judgment was to *begin*
at the house of God," so we see it verified, in *her*
becoming the *first* victim of the spoliators ; for " the
things which may be shaken must be removed, to
make way for those which never may be shaken."
Therefore, much as we may and *ought to prize these*
blessings of church privileges and ordinances, whilst
we possess them, whatever their imperfections may
be, as " the sealed fountains and gardens inclosed,'
wherein so many trees of righteousness have " been
planted in the house of the Lord, and have flou-
rished in the courts of the house of our God ;"
still it is too possible, that we may live to see all
these hallowed places of resort, and cherished ones
of memory, scattered to the four winds of heaven;
and therefore we must seek to be possessed of *a confidence* which we can carry in our own bosom, when
we are called to go forth with our life in our hands,

stripped of all those accessories which have hitherto
been the props on which we leant for support; one
so defensive in its nature, as to prove like an ark to
us, to enable us to ride out the storm, and bear us
in safety over the troubled waters of this world,
when the fountains of the great deep of *human society* are broken up, and destruction and desolation
reign around us; and one so indestructible in its
properties, as to enable us " to glorify God in the
fires with which He shall speedily try all the earth,"
when " He shall take away the filth of the daugh-
ters of Zion, by the spirit of judgment, and by the
spirit of burning"—" for, in those days, a man shall
not look to the altars the work of his hands, neither have respect to that which his fingers have
made : for his strong cities shall be a forsaken
bough," to which none shall dare to cling for support, and we shall all find, who live to encounter it,
that " the name of the Lord," and that only " is a
strong tower, the righteous runneth into *it*, and *is
safe;*" for, " O how great is thy goodness, which
thou hast laid up for them that fear thee, which
thou hast wrought for them that trust in thee, before the sons of men ; thou shalt hide them in the
secret of thy presence from the pride of man;
thou shalt keep them secretly in a 'pavilion from
the strife of tongues."

Let none " lay the flattering unction to their
souls," that because our Lord has said, " The gates

of hell shall never prevail against his church,' that therefore *their* favourite church on earth, since it possesses those qualifications which in their eyes constitute its distinctive claim to *this* appellation, shall remain impregnable: as this promise, which relates to the church spiritual, no mere temporal church may dare so arrogate to herself as to say, her mountain stands so strong she shall never be moved; for however scriptural in doctrine, primitive in origin, and unpolluted in ordinances she may be, still none can allege they are therefore placed beyond the risk of ever falling from the faith, or out of the reach of the danger of ever becoming so infected with error, or tainted with heresy, as that her candlestick shall never be removed from its place, as happened to the seven primitive churches, whose foundations, indisputably, *were* laid by the apostle's own hands, who possessed the miraculous gifts of the Holy Ghost, and amongst whom our Lord describes Himself as walking, and holding their stars in His right hand.

If some of them entirely lost their privileges, and our Lord threatened *all* with the same fate, unless they strengthened the things that remained, and except they repented of their deeds, no existing church, surely, will venture to affirm *she* possesses *greater* means of security than *they* did ? The mystical and spiritual church of Christ *shall, indeed,* experience the truth of this promise of her divine

Master, in its fullest and widest sense, as not one of *her* living stones shall Satan be permitted *to* lay a finger upon for their displacement in the holy temple, though he *may* be suffered to wreak his vengeance upon " every earthly tabernacle of *this* building ;" and the efforts now making by the leading reformers of the day are too open, too powerful, and alas ! *too successful,* to leave any doubts upon our minds, that those in this land *have* been for a time given into his hands ; as, besides the efforts made for their destruction from without, the spirit of infatuation which guides their councils within, warns us the hour of their departure is at hand !

The church of Scotland has, by a suicidal act, hastened her doom ; for feeling that, from a fault in her original constitution, she had lost the affections of the higher classes, in whose hands her temporalities are placed, she has thrown herself into the hands of the lower classes ; and, by an act of gross injustice, and in open defiance of the laws of the land, has transferred the rights of the one party into the hands of the other ; exasperating *their* feelings of indifference into indignation and disgust ; whilst she will find that this attempt to propitiate the favour of the mob will fail (as all such attempts have *ever* failed) to secure their gratitude, and gain their affections ; who will only use the power she has conferred on them, as they have done in every other instance, for her destruction. The church of England, again, assailed on the one hand by the aggressive assaults of the infidel body that would wish to sweep *her* from the face of the earth, who, they find, is the greatest impediment to the success of their efforts; and by the encroaching attempts of Dissenters without her pale, to share in those advantages within it, which the wisdom of our forefathers fenced round for *her* benefit alone; and seeing the great dragon, which their sad experience of its evils had bound with a chain, let loose once again upon her, and rearing its crested head in an attitude of fierce attack; in place of putting into the hands of her sons those only weapons of sound scripture truth, which can alone enable them to preserve *themselves* and defend *her* at such a moment, is found, while the enemy is, as it were, scaling the walls,. burnishing up all her tarnished ornaments, and restoring obsolete ceremonies; and trying to enforce a blind veneration for non-essentials, and a bigoted revival of antiquated customs, more befitting the dark ages of superstition than those of advanced knowledge, and of impatience of all restraints. And in place of holding up the light of a purer and sounder faith, and a simpler mode of worship, as the most striking contrast to convince every reflecting and candid mind of her superiority, and to

disenthral all those who have been ensnared by
Rome's gaudy splendour, is entering into a weak
and most unworthy rivalry with her adversary, and
is striving to outdo her in these things! Satan having, as it were, cast the mantle of delusion over her,
as the Spanish mattadore does to the bull, leaving
her to buffet with it, while he slips round to wound
her in a more defenceless part.

Let not such as exult with a shout of triumph
over the destruction which seems ready to over-
whelm all existing institutions, as opening up the
prospect of the coming in of *their* fancied visions of
glory, and the restoration of the fabled golden age,
which their heathen wishes look forward to, and
who think the removal of these obstructions to it
will prepare the way for that season of spiritual
enfranchisement, which will fully develope all their
socialist, chartist, and liberal plans, which they expect will regenerate the world, after the fashion of
their ungodly and infidel model, flatter themselves
that the hour of the fulfilment of all *their* hopes is
near. Ah! little do they know that their hasten-
ing on of this grand political earthquake has helped
to purify the moral atmosphere for " the restitution
of all things," under a holier and happier form.
Little do they imagine, that their subversion of all
existing institutions is but the carrying out the
purposes of Almighty God for their *own* destruc-

R

tion, ultimately, whose word has gone forth, " I
will overturn, overturn, overturn it, and it shall be
no more until He comes *whose right it is ;* and I
will give it to Him : and the government shall be
upon His shoulders; for the Lord shall be king over all
the earth.   And of the *increase* of *His* government
and *peace* there shall be no end, upon the throne
of David, to order it and to establish it with judgment and with justice, from henceforth, even for
ever and ever !" And that they who have broken down
the walls of our ever-hallowed establishment, have
but been removing the scaffolding, to allow of the
real building to appear ; and have been but uncon-
sciously assisting to establish a regularly consti-
tuted and rightly organized hierarchy on earth,
resembling that which they have destroyed, in most
of its features save in its possessing those principles
of perfection and endurance which *it* wanted, and
which will insure its efficiency and secure its permanency for ever,—" When the Lord our God shall
reign on mount Zion, and before all His ancients
gloriously, and when He shall sit as a priest upon
His throne, and His people shall be kings and ˌriests
unto Him, in *that city* which *hath* foundations, whose
builder and maker is God ; and the name of that
city from that day shall be, the Lord is there !"

   As we are not left without hopes, by the expo-
sitors of prophecy, that those churches which have

kept the faith unsullied, may have a subordinate part allotted to them in the new dispensation, " the virgins," which, as the fellows of the Bride, shall bear her company, and as appendages to her glory, with joy and gladness shall enter into the king's palaces with her; so those who prefer our national Zion above their chief joy, and who owe their own souls to her, must reflect with thankfulness, that if there is one church more than another which possesses in itself those integral and preservative elements which shall enable it to stand the test of that " fire which is to try every man's work of what sort it is," or to arise, like the phœnix, from the ashes of universal conflagration, that church is the Church of England. If we are bid " to rise up before the hoary head," much more may sentiments of respectful awe impress us, as we lift up the eyes of our regard upon her venerable structure, which, in antiquity of origin, orthodoxy of doctrine, and purity of ordinances, can challenge comparison with every church in existence upon earth ; for without pushing her claim into that debateable ground which is the subject of so much controversy at the present day, we may yet safely assert she possesses claims upon our respect and obedience, which rest on a foundation none can controvert. We can trace up her pure stream to the primitive fountain-head of apostolic times, long before Rome had cast in the poison of

her " golden cup of abominations and of filthiness"
into it; and though, from the very fact of its re-
mote date, it is not easy to say who were the human
instruments employed to publish the Gospel first in
this island, the weight which the British church had
in the early councils—that, for instance, at Arles in
Gaul, in the year of our Lord 314, which was attended by three British bishops—that held at
Rimini, in the year 359, by the Emperor Constan-
tine, when their poverty forms not the least interesting feature of the story, in their being obliged
to live at the emperor's expense; as well as the
honourable mention of their attestation to the doctrines contained in the Nicene Creed and that of
St. Athanasius, composed to meet the prevalent
heresies of the times, which Athanasius alludes to
in his Apology against the Arians, written in 350;
and Hilary's address to them in his book de Syno-
dis, written in 358—are all proofs that St. Austin's
visit to Britain, in 596, was to repair the decayed
walls only, and not to lay the foundation stone of
our national Zion, as Rome ostentatiously asserts.
And though we must with shame confess, that,
unlike the blue waters of that river which keeps
its bright tint unsullied in passing through a
lake, we, on the contrary, were at length so
blended with that dead sea which soon overspread
all the earth, as to become inconspicuous as a wit-

ness to the truth ; still we were amongst the first of
the churches, which came out, and were separated"
from Rome, at the Reformation, and that submitted
to have our polluted waters filtered through the
purifying minds of the reformers.

And to those who undertook the task in this land
we owe it, that whilst they scrupulously discarded
every particle of Rome's deleterious ingredients,
the venerable framers of our Liturgy, with a magnanimity, forbearance, and discretion, which formed a
striking contrast to the indiscriminating destruction
of others, preserved for our benefit all those hoarded
stores of pious wisdom, which the industry and
learning of our ancestors had accumulated; and
restored to our use everything sanctioned by the
authority of Scripture, and sanctified by the example of the primitive church, which could stand the
test of Scripture, and bore not the stamp of Rome's
apostate hand. And in place of throwing us upon
the resources of raw inexperience, and leaving us
to draw upon the meagre scrip of scanty modern
acquirements, presented us thus, in our creeds,
articles, homilies, and, above all, in our church services, with a condensed but complete body of divinity,
which has ever since proved like a fence of spears
around the church's sacred enclosure, to ward off
infidels, as well as a searching test within her walls,
to bring to light all latent heresy : for as Hannah

More justly remarks, the propounder of heresy from the pulpit must ever have his error met and contradicted by the desk below him; and which provision of a regular Liturgy, in place of leaving us at the mercy of the varying talents of such leaders as futurity should hereafter place over God's heritages, provided against our ever suffering from the wants of such, in the individual appointed over us, by a form of prayer, to which men's talent can add nothing, and their want of it take nothing away from us, whilst, by leaving the pulpit free, it left us an opportunity of always benefiting from any such gifts as should fall to our lot. What the advantage of this form of prayer is, they best can know who, among all the varying trials of life, and its vicissitudes of joy and grief, have ever found how beautifully and completely it was adapted to meet its every state of feeling; but which Simeon of Cambridge has remarked, those only, who could hear all the extemporary effusions poured forth in all the dissenting chapels of the land, could know " what reason they had to fall down and thank God on their knees for having granted it to them."

Nay, not only did the care of our reformers for us extend to these intrinsic blessings, but also to preserving for us the very hallowed cisterns which the providence of our forefathers had hewn out to hold the precious waters of life for us in this country;

for they, in place of waging war against the inoffen-
sive stones and mortar, contented themselves with
simply cleansing these from Rome's defilements,
leaving us the sublime satisfaction, as the pious
Cecil observes, of reflecting, as we tread under the
roofs of our ancient cathedrals and churches—

" Where through the long-drawn aisle and fretted vault,
The pealing anthem swells the note of praise."—(GRAY.)

That " Thou art the King of glory, O Christ,
Thou art the everlasting Son of the Father," has
ascended from the lips of our fathers, and of our
father's fathers, through countless generations.

A church which may be emphatically called the
poor man's church, as no other has more largely
contributed to his benefit, and more liberally provided for his wants, than it has done; and such
ample room for his accommodation, where, " without
money and without price," he finds abundant means
for his soul's salvation placed within his reach : in
an opportunity for the public worship of his God,
and the free and more frequent reception of the
holy sacraments, " duly administered," than he can
find anywhere else. And, above all, where he is
furnished with a regular and larger portion of God's
unadulterated word, read in his hearing, four chapters
entire every sabbath, and large portions of the
Psalms and of other parts of the Bible selected for
him, besides that appointed for week-days, so that

"they who occupy the room of the unlearned," even
if so ignorant as to be unable to read their Bibles,
" if they have ears to hear may hear," and " receive into an honest and good heart the incorruptible word of life, which is able to save their
souls," leaving all such without excuse if they
wander from the fold of their national church,
because of the incompetency of their shepherd,
seeing they have been made independent of this by
having all the means of grace so placed in their
own power as no defects in the mere human instrument appointed to administer them can render
invalid and ineffectual, save through their own fault
and negligence.

A church, too, as admirably adapted for the higher
classes of society also, as the clergy taken from
among their ranks remain as the preservative salt,
even when they do not spread, as they were intended to do, as " the little leaven, leavening all the
lump " of human society.   And though, from the
tendency in men's minds to pervert the best of
things, these good ends have been too often frus-
trated, and their plans defeated, and this wise ar-
rangement has tended oftener to secularize the
clergy, than the clergy have succeeded in spiritu-
alising the world around them; still it has advantages that may well redeem it from unqualified
censure in the eyes of all candid and dispassionate

men, as to their sacred and salutary influence it is
owing, that our Hales, and Boyles, and Newtons, and
Chathams, attained a height of moral, as well as of intellectual eminence, that rendered them burning and
shining lights to all lands as well as their own : and
to the thickly-set resident gentry of highly culti-
vated minds and good morals this insures in England, we owe it that the homes and hearths of our
aristocracy have been the centre of a high-toned
virtue, literary elegance, and domestic happiness, to
an extent unknown in foreign lands. If our ever-
venerated church understood, at least in this her
day, the things which belong to her peace and to her
preservation, and wherein lies the strength of her
honourable position, and sought to improve these her
legitimate and hitherto most successful means of
doing good in her generation, we should not fear
for her " though the earth be moved, and though
the hills be carried into the midst of the sea." Did
she show her clergy what were their high duties
towards both ranks, and enforced on them the performance of them, ejecting from her bosom all such
as neglected them, and disgraced their high calling
and profession, and brought dishonour upon her, by
prostituting the means she has given them for the
fulfilment of these duties, and maintaining that
standing of respectability befitting their office, in
following the sports of the field and the follies of the

ball-room; and in place of entrenching herself within the mere outworks of rites and ceremonies, by which means she is disgusting the truly pious and spiritually-minded of her flock, and sealing the destruction of the formalists, by lulling their consciences asleep in a mere round of carnal duties,— were she to be " instant in season and out of season, in reproving, rebuking, exhorting, with all long-suffering and doctrine, and instructing her members * in the spiritual nature, the doctrinal importance, and scriptural correctness of *all* her services, which need not the apochrypha of tradition to add to their weight—if she would show them how their interests, both here and hereafter, are so inseparably bound up with her existence, that their national prosperity and glory are identified with *her* preservation even, who from the cradle to the grave watches over them individually and collectively, receiving them into her fold at baptism, consecrating them afresh and setting them more solemnly apart for God's service at confirmation, ere she admits them to her still higher privileges—strengthens them after this by her oft-repeated communion of the body and blood of their Lord—humbles them by her Lent services, and elevates and cheers them by her Easter and Christmas festivals— recalling thus forcibly to their memories, annually, the death and

* This, it is true, a large body of her clergy are now doing.

passion, the glorious resurrection and ascension of their only Lord and Saviour Jesus Christ—bends over them in sickness, with her soothing but most impressive " prayers for the sick,"—and finally commits the body of each member of her communion to the grave, " in the sure and certain hope of a resurrection to eternal life," in one of the most sublime, touching, and soul-exalting services ever composed by the pen of man, or ever heard by mortal ear on earth.

And if she, besides all this, while resisting the unchristian efforts of our present rulers for the irreligious education of her children, took away every pretence and every excuse for their interference, by leaving not one child within her reach uneducated in sound, wholesome *religious* principles, she would rear around her an enlightened and intelligent population, as a valuable accession to her strength, besides binding all her sons firmer and faster to her side, and produce a re-action in her favour that would more than undo the mischief of her enemies, and more than fulfil the hopes of her friends.

If her clergy, besides, sought to oppose the antidote of their healing and holy ministrations among the higher orders, to the infectious influence of continental intercourse, and the importation into our literature of all the impurities of France,

" All monstrous, all prodigious things, abominable, unutterable,"

with which our own press vies too in an unholy
:mulation, trying if possible to outstrip it, in cover-
·ng our tables with everything that can corrupt the
nind, and debase the understanding, and used
their earnest exertions to try and stem the tide of
rapid demoralization among the lower classes;—
then should we see her once more "look forth like
the morning, fair as the moon, clear as the sun, and
terrible as an army with banners." But if she per-
sists, instead, in the vain strife with Rome, in seeking to court men by solicitations addressed to their
senses chiefly, and in contests about priority of
dates and endless genealogies, which minister to
strife, not to godly edifying, Rome will soon beat
her with her own weapons, in the use of which she
has been too long practised to fear defeat. Let her
exalt her crest ever so high, Rome will overtop her
in lofty assumption of dignity and pretensions to
authority, who will yield the palm to none in arro-
gancy and superstition. Let her assert what dominion she pleases over the consciences of men,
Rome need fear no competition in *this*, backed as
she is by a Jesuitical priesthood, and the terrors of
the Inquisition. Let her spread what snares she will
for the senses of men, here her adversary has every
advantage, and need fear no rival; nay, will thank
her cordially for holding her up as a model, in things
in which she must ever have the pre-eminence,

who is not hemmed in by those barriers and restrictions which Protestant *prejudices* present, even when Protestant *principles* are on the decline.

Our church would do well, at this moment, to learn a lesson of those who war with other weapons than she ever can use, as all who are skilled in the tactics of carnal warfare can tell her, that in proportion as an army increases in rules of punctilious etiquette and attention to externals, it declines in vital energy and moral strength; and, in fact, it is in the memories of some even of the present generation, that whilst that miserable system prevailed, adopted by short-sighted minds, who thought that the perfection of an army consisted in uniformity of dress and accoutrements, our arms were tarnished in more quarters of the globe than one, till a more rational one, exploding all these narrow-minded rules, and infusing a spirit-stirring principle into men's minds, led our troops on to a determination of purpose, and an energy of action, that not only retrieved the honour of our arms, but raised our national credit to a height of glory and renown, under the great captain of the day, unknown in the annals of fame before, even of our great and illustrious land.

But whether our church may or may not do *her* duty in these alarming and critical times, the duty of individuals is clear, and remains the same. She has *her* responsibility, and must give account to her Head for all that she does, and for all that she leaves undone. And we *have ours*, from which she can neither release nor absolve us; to our own Master, each must separately stand or fall, not as one of a body, nor as members of any sect, or party, or church, but we must alone appear before the judgment-seat of God, to give account to " Him who has been about our path, and about our bed, and who has spied out all our ways, for lo, there is not a word in our tongue, but thou, O Lord, knowest it altogether." And each one of us, now-a-days, with the lamp of divine truth in our hands, (the holy Scriptures,) and the Holy Spirit, to " guide us into all truth," "*given to every man*, to profit withal, that " our ears may hear a word behind us, say-ing, This is the way, walk ye in it," (Isa. xxx. 21,) " when ye turn aside to the right hand, and when ye turn aside to the left," are left wholly without excuse if we do not find out the way in which we should go, and having found it, do not walk therein with 'a perfect heart; knowing, that He who shall come to be our judge, has said, " And all the churches shall know that I am He that searches *the reins and the hearts :* and I will give unto every one of you according to your works." " Wherefore, beloved, seeing that ye look for such things, be diligent that ye may be found of Him, without spot and blameless."

Now, " unto Him that is able to keep you from falling, and to present you faultless before the presence of His glory with exceeding joy, to the only wise God our Saviour, be glory, majesty, dominion, and power, both now and ever." Amen.

"Cast not away, therefore, your *Confidence*, which hath great recompence of reward!" (Heb. x. 35.)

THE END

LONDON:
PRINTED BY IBOTSON AND PALMER,
SAVOY STREET.

Breinigsville, PA USA
17 January 2011
253499BV00004B/52/P

9 781104 637040